the COMPACT HISTORY
of the CATHOLIC CHURCH

the COMPACT HISTORY *of the* CATHOLIC CHURCH

ALAN SCHRECK, PH.D.

SERVANT
BOOKS

PUBLISHED BY ST. ANTHONY MESSENGER PRESS
CINCINNATI, OHIO

Cover and book design by Jennifer Tibbits
Cover photo copyright azneye23/istockphoto.com

LIBRARY OF CONGRESS CATALOGING-IN-PUBLICATION DATA

Schreck, Alan.
The compact history of the Catholic Church / Alan Schreck. — Rev. ed.
p. cm.
Includes bibliographical references and index.
ISBN 978-0-86716-879-2 (pbk. : alk. paper) 1. Catholic Church—
History. 2. Church history. I. Title.
BX945.3.S38 2009
282.09—dc22

2008046327

ISBN 978-0-86716-879-2

Published by Servant Books,
an imprint of St. Anthony Messenger Press
28 W. Liberty St.
Cincinnati, OH 45202
www.ServantBooks.org

Printed in the United States of America.

Printed on acid-free paper.

09 10 11 12 13 5 4 3 2 1

contents

This book came into being when Father Fio Mascarenhas, S.J., then-chairman of the International Catholic Charismatic Renewal Office (ICCRO) in Rome, asked me to write a series of simple lessons on the history of the Catholic Church as a follow-up to the Life in the Spirit Seminars, especially for use in Third World countries.[1] The original manuscript of this text was divided into eight sessions, to be presented by a leader to a group of people.

The reader should be aware of the original purpose of this work. It provides a nontechnical, introductory overview of the Catholic understanding of the Church and its history. I hope that the reader finds it genuinely helpful for this purpose.

I would like to acknowledge the generous support and assistance of the ICCRO staff in Rome, where I wrote the bulk of this book during two weeks in March 1986. (I completed this updated version in early 2008.) I would also like to thank my wife, Nancy, and my children Paul, Jeanne, Mark, Margaret and Peter for praying and sacrificially supporting me in my writing.

Finally, all praise, glory and honor is due to God, who out of his great love formed a people to be his own and who continually guides his Church as it goes its pilgrim way, until it reaches its glorious completion in the fullness of God's eternal kingdom!

the CATHOLIC UNDERSTANDING
of the CHURCH

What is Christianity all about? What is Catholicism about? Is it only a philosophy of life, a set of teachings to memorize or rules to live by?

No, Christianity is not an idea but a *reality* that exists in human history. Christianity is about

- a *person*, Jesus Christ, the "founder" of Christianity;
- a *people* that God has formed on the earth;
- a *way of life* that God has given his people.

This book will look at the nature and the history of the *people* that God has called forth and formed on the earth: the people of God.

How do we know that Christianity and Catholicism are primarily about God's forming a people to be his own? Let us look at the Bible, the inspired written account of God's work and revelation.

GOD'S PLAN:

To Form a People

The Old Testament is the story of the *people* that God was calling forth and teaching in order to bring the human race back into friendship with himself after the rebellion of Adam and Eve. Abraham was the human "father" of this people because of his faithful response to God's call. God entered into a covenant with Abraham, a solemn agreement, which was the basis of the relationship between God and his people. Christians call this covenant with Abraham and the Hebrew (Jewish) people the old covenant because it was later replaced by a new covenant, as was predicted by Jeremiah the prophet:

> Behold, the days are coming, says the LORD, when I will make a new covenant with the house of Israel and the house of Judah, not like the covenant which I made with their fathers when I took them by the hand to bring them out of the land of Egypt, my covenant which they broke.
>
> …But this is the covenant which I will make with the house of Israel after those days, says the LORD: I will put my law within them, and I will write it upon their hearts; and I will be their God, and they shall be my people. And no longer shall each man teach his neighbor and each his brother, saying, "Know the LORD," for they shall all know me, from the least of them to the greatest, says the LORD; for I will forgive their iniquity, and I will remember their sin no more. (Jeremiah 31:31–32, 33–34)

The Old Testament tells us the story of God's mercy and patience in forming and teaching this old covenant people, called the nation of Israel, or the Jewish people. The prophet Jeremiah reminds us, however, that this old covenant was limited and imperfect. The way of life that God gave the people of the old covenant was expressed in the Law, especially the Ten Commandments, which God gave the people through Moses; but the people often broke the Law because it was only external; it was not "written upon their hearts."

The old covenant was not the final plan of God. God was preparing the people of the old covenant for something else— something better. God was preparing them for the coming of the Messiah, the "anointed one" of God who would establish the new covenant, which would bring God's work to completion and fulfillment. The New Testament continues the story of God's forming a *people*, the people of God of the new covenant.

God had a tremendous surprise for his people. The Messiah that the people of the old covenant awaited was not to be an ordinary human being or even a divine messenger like an angel. The Messiah of Israel would be God the Son, the Second Person of the Blessed Trinity, who would assume our human nature and live among us as a man—Jesus of Nazareth. Jesus was the Christ, the Messiah, the Savior sent by God the Father to bring the old covenant to completion and to form a new people, the people of the new covenant.

At his Last Supper with his apostles, Jesus took the cup of wine and said, "This cup which is poured out for you is the new covenant in my blood" (Luke 22:20). Jesus' blood, shed on the cross of Calvary, sealed and began a new covenant, a new relationship between God and man. The blood of Jesus shed on the cross brought forgiveness for all the sins of humankind.

As the prophet Jeremiah said, "I [God] will forgive their iniquity, and I will remember their sin no more" (Jeremiah 31:34).

The death and resurrection of Jesus began the life of a new people of God, the people of the new covenant. This people believed that Jesus was truly the Savior sent by God; they believed that God had confirmed this by raising Jesus from death—by the Resurrection. This people then received new life through the Holy Spirit, whom Jesus had promised to send to them. Jesus said: "I have yet many things to say to you, but you cannot bear them now. When the Spirit of truth comes, he will guide you into all the truth; for he will not speak on his own authority, but whatever he hears he will speak, and he will declare to you the things that are to come" (John 16:12–13).

The fulfillment of Jesus' promise to send the Holy Spirit came on the Day of Pentecost, a major Jewish feast, when 120 followers of Jesus were praying together in Jerusalem, and the Holy Spirit rested on each of them like "tongues as of fire" (Acts 2:3). This was the fulfillment of Jeremiah's prophecy that God's law would be put within them and "written upon their hearts." As the apostle Paul wrote to the church in Rome, "The law of the Spirit of life in Christ Jesus has set me free from the law of sin and death" (Romans 8:2).

The Holy Spirit also enables the new people of God to know God personally and to understand his will and guidance from within, rather than as an external set of rules. Truly, the people of God who have received Jesus' promise of the Holy Spirit have no need to ask others, "Who is God?" for they all know God, from the least of them to the greatest, as Jeremiah prophesied (see Jeremiah 31:34).

GOD'S NEW COVENANT PEOPLE:

The Church

The Church is the people of God of the new covenant! They are the ones who believe that Jesus is the Messiah, the Christ, the Son of God who was raised from the dead. They are the people who have received the Holy Spirit, the Third Person of God, into their hearts and through the Spirit have the life and power of God within them.

What is the *name* of this new people of God? The New Testament calls the followers of Jesus "the saints" (see Ephesians 1:1; Philippians 1:1; Colossians 1:2), "God's beloved" (Romans 1:7), "Christians" (Acts 11:26) and followers of "the Way" (Acts 19:23). However, the most common name for God's people of the new covenant, the name that has lasted over many centuries, is the *Church*. Although the word *church* is found most frequently in the Acts of the Apostles and the various letters of the New Testament, even Jesus is reported to have used this word for his people. We read in the Gospel of Matthew Jesus' words to Peter: "And I tell you, you are Peter, and on this rock I will build my church, and the powers of death [literally, 'the gates of hades'] shall not prevail against it" (Matthew 16:18).

Jesus called the Church "my church." He is the founder of the Church. He said the Church would never be destroyed: "The powers of death shall not prevail against it." Why? Because Jesus promised to remain with his Church until the end of time. Jesus assured his apostles immediately before his ascension into heaven, "I am with you always, to the close of the age" (Matthew 28:20).

Jesus will never leave or abandon his Church because he *loves* it to the point of dying for it on the cross. The Letter to the Ephesians beautifully tells us of the love of Christ for the Church when it speaks of the Church as the "bride of Christ":

> For the husband is the head of the wife as Christ is the head of the church, his body, and is himself its Savior.... Husbands, love your wives, as Christ loved the church and gave himself up for her, that he might sanctify her, having cleansed her ..., that he might present the church to himself in splendor, without spot or wrinkle or any such thing, that she might be holy and without blemish.... This mystery is a profound one, and I am saying that it refers to Christ and the church. (Ephesians 5:23, 25–27, 32)

The fulfillment of Jesus' work of preparing his bride, the Church, for himself is described in the book of Revelation. Christ, the Lamb of God, weds his bride, the Church, at the end of time: "'The marriage of the Lamb has come, and his Bride has made herself ready; it was granted her to be clothed with fine linen, bright and pure'—for the fine linen is the righteous deeds of the saints" (Revelation 19:7–8).

This is what God is doing in human history. He is forming a people, a bride for his Son Jesus Christ, and purifying the Church so it will be ready when Christ comes again in glory. We know that this work of purification is not yet complete. Although we can see "the righteous deeds of the saints," we also know that there is still sin in the Church, for Christ came not to call the righteous but sinners (see Luke 5:32). Yet in spite of the evident sin and weakness in the Church, Christ still loves it enough to die on the cross for his people, the Church.

It is evident that the history of the Church is marked by both sin and weakness as well as by the grace and protection of God. This is because the Church is not only a divine reality but also human, like Jesus himself. Unlike Jesus, however, the Church is not totally free from sin but is in the process in each age of being freed from sin and being conformed to the image of Jesus, the head of the Church.

The Gospels are full of stories of sinners being redeemed—prostitutes, the self-righteous and even apostles like Peter. All of them needed mercy and forgiveness. What is true in the Gospels is true of the Church throughout history.

In spite of the sin in the Church today and in history, Christians are called not to criticize or to sit in judgment over the Church but to love the Church as Jesus does. We, as members of the Church, are sinners ourselves. Yet Jesus loves us enough to die for us to free us from our sin and weakness. The same is true of the Church as a whole. Despite its sinfulness Christ loves the Church and looks upon it as his beloved bride. God is at work to purify and renew his people, his Church. Each of us should say, with Cardinal Suenens, "I love the Church, wrinkles and all!"[1] We love the Church in spite of imperfections, because Jesus Christ loves it and died to redeem his people.

When we say "the Church," what do we mean? Do we mean the Catholic Church or a universal church of all who believe in Jesus Christ? We cannot answer this question completely in this chapter, but we can briefly look at four characteristics or essential "marks" of the Church that are expressed in the Nicene Creed (AD 381): "We believe in one, holy, catholic and apostolic Church." In doing this and in examining in later chapters the history of the Church from a Catholic perspective, we will better understand the meaning of the word *church* as it is understood from the Catholic Christian viewpoint.

THE CHURCH IS ONE

The authors of the New Testament understood there was only *one* Church, one people of God of the new covenant. Although the apostle Paul wrote to the "churches of Galatia" (Galatians 1:2) and the "church of God which is at Corinth" (1 Corinthians 1:2), he knew that these local gatherings of Christians were all part of the one Church of Jesus Christ, much as a single corporation or business might have many plants or branches in different locations.

Paul himself was a strong defender of the unity of the Church. He corrected the Christians in Corinth for dividing into opposed groups with different leaders (see 1 Corinthians 1:10–13). He wrote to the Christians in Ephesus to be "eager to maintain the unity of the Spirit in the bond of peace" (Ephesians 4:3), insisting that "there is one body and one Spirit,…one hope…, one Lord, one faith, one baptism, one God and Father of us all" (Ephesians 4:4–6).

The Acts of the Apostles records two instances in which disputes among Christians threatened to divide the early Church. In Acts 6 the primitive Church in Jerusalem underwent a serious disagreement between Hebrew-speaking and Greek-speaking Christian converts from Judaism concerning the distribution of food to the widows in the Church. Acts 15 reports the most serious disagreement that challenged the unity of the Church in the first century: the question of whether gentiles needed to be circumcised according to Jewish law before they could become Christians. In both cases the disputes were resolved peacefully by meetings, or "councils," of the leaders ("elders") of the Church, who found resolutions to these questions through the guidance of the Holy Spirit. Instead of dividing into two "churches" when serious disagreements arose, the early Christians sought earnestly to preserve the oneness of the Church.

The early Christians valued unity so much because Jesus did. In the account of the Last Supper in the Gospel of John, Jesus prayed for the unity of his followers: "that they may all be one; even as thou, Father, art in me, and I in thee, that they also may be in us, so that the world may believe that thou hast sent me" (John 17:21).

The basis of this unity is love: "By this all men will know that you are my disciples, if you have love for one another" (John 13:35). The love of Christ is the basis and source of the unity of his people, the Church. The Holy Spirit is often viewed as the love that unites Christians, just as he is the bond of unity between the Father and the Son in the Blessed Trinity.

The Catholic Church has always stressed the oneness or unity of the Church. We understand this unity as both an *invisible* unity of love, the "unity of the Holy Spirit," and also a *visible* unity that is expressed in the outward forms of the Church: leaders, creeds and other beliefs and sacraments, for example. Authority and leaders in the Church are a gift of God to protect and preserve the Church's visible unity. Catholics believe that Jesus intended a Church united both in spirit and in outward expression. The invisible work of love and the Holy Spirit produces visible, outward unity among God's people.

THE CHURCH IS CATHOLIC

We have just seen that there was originally one Church of Jesus Christ. The term *catholic* was first used to describe this one Church in a letter of an early Christian martyr and bishop, Ignatius of Antioch. He wrote on his way to martyrdom in Rome in the year AD 110: "Where the bishop is present, there let the congregation gather, just as where Jesus Christ is, there is the catholic church."[2] His point was that just as each local branch of the Church found its visible focus of unity in the bishop, the *whole* Church, the catholic Church, found its focus of unity in Jesus Christ. Thus the phrase "catholic Church" originally meant "the whole Church" or the "universal Church"—the Church of Jesus Christ spread throughout the whole known world. The phrase "catholic Church" also came to indicate the Church that taught the whole truth of Christianity. Thus *catholic* became synonymous with *orthodox*—embracing all Christian truth.

Today also it is true that the Church of Jesus Christ is "catholic." It is universal. It embraces all peoples, nations and cultures. It expresses the full truth of Christianity. The people of God of the new covenant is to be a people including all who respond in faith to the Good News of God's love in Jesus Christ.

However, we know that today the term *catholic* also refers to a specific group of believers in Jesus, the Catholic Church. How did this come about?

As Christianity spread through the Roman Empire and beyond in the second and third centuries after Christ, certain small groups began to disagree with the beliefs of the way of life of this universal Church. These groups—the Montanists,

Gnostics, Novationists, Donatists and others—considered themselves the true church of Jesus Christ because they thought they alone faithfully preserved the true Christian teaching and way of life. In order to distinguish it from these small groups, the term *Catholic Church* began to be applied to the large, universal Church from which these smaller groups divided. So *Catholic* was used as a formal name for this great, universal body of Christians spread throughout the known world, which also claimed to possess the fullness of Christian truth.

An example of this is the prayer of Monica, the mother of Augustine, a brilliant young man born in North Africa in AD 354. While Augustine was still a pagan searching for truth, Monica prayed fervently that her son would become a "Catholic Christian" before she died.[3] Her prayer was answered. Not only did Augustine become a "Catholic" Christian, but he also eventually became a Catholic bishop and one of the greatest theologians of the Catholic Church.

Today Catholics look at the history of their Church and realize that if there is to be *one* Church of Jesus Christ, this Church must also be catholic or universal: embracing all peoples, languages, nations and cultures and teaching the fullness of Christian truth. The Catholic Church is such a body, being the largest and most extensive united body of Christians in the world and claiming to embrace all authentic Christian belief.

THE CHURCH IS HOLY

What do we mean when we profess that the Church is holy? Many people think it means the Church is perfect or without sin. That cannot be true because Christ came to call and save sinners; the Church is full of sinners, us!

Holy literally means "set apart." God is holy because he is "set apart" from all his creatures, from everything he has made. God can share his holiness with his creation by setting apart certain people, places and things for himself and his purposes. The Church is holy because it contains people whom God has set apart to be his own people, chosen by God for his purposes.

The Church's being set apart does not mean being separated from the world but rather being *consecrated* to God and his purposes in the world. As Jesus himself prayed in his "high priestly prayer": "I consecrate myself, that they also may be consecrated in truth" (John 17:19). As the apostle Peter proclaimed to the Church in his first letter: "You are a chosen race, a royal priesthood, a holy nation, God's own people, that you may declare the wonderful deeds of him who called you out of darkness into his marvelous light. Once you were no people but now you are God's people; once you had not received mercy but now you have received mercy" (1 Peter 2:9–10).

The Church is holy not because of its own perfection or merits but only because it is the people whom God has set apart, consecrated and chosen to receive his mercy. This mercy is given through the passion, death and resurrection of Jesus Christ. Catholics thank God for the privilege of being called to be part of this holy nation, the Church.

THE CHURCH IS APOSTOLIC

This holy Church is not a private club or association. Before his ascension Jesus commanded his followers: "Go therefore and make disciples of all nations, baptizing them in the name of the

Father and of the Son and of the Holy Spirit, teaching them to observe all that I have commanded you" (Matthew 28:19–20).

Jesus not only commanded his followers to spread the good news of his resurrection to others but also gave them the Holy Spirit to empower them for this mission: "You shall receive power when the Holy Spirit has come upon you; and you shall be my witnesses in Jerusalem and in all Judea and Samaria and to the end of the earth" (Acts 1:8).

"The Church is apostolic" means it carries on the mission of the apostles to spread the Good News of Jesus Christ to every nation and people, to "declare the wonderful deeds of him who called you out of darkness into his marvelous light" (1 Peter 2:9). Each Christian is called to be a missionary, an evangelizer, because the Church itself is missionary and evangelistic.

"The Church is apostolic" has one other important meaning. The Letter to the Ephesians states the Church is "built upon the foundation of the apostles and prophets, Christ Jesus himself being the cornerstone" (Ephesians 2:20). Being "apostolic" means being built on the foundation of the apostles. Catholic Christians recognize the bishops, including the bishop of Rome, the pope, as carrying on the leadership and the authority of the apostles throughout the history of the Church. "The Church is apostolic" means that the authority and mission of the apostles did not end when they died; the Church continues to build on the foundation of the apostles and prophets through the ministry of their successors, the bishops, throughout history.

The Catholic understanding of the call to be a bishop is that there is an unbroken line of succession that can be traced through history from the present Catholic bishops back to the apostles of Jesus themselves. The bishops, therefore, have a special responsibility to carry on the apostles' work of preaching, teaching, guiding, feeding and shepherding God's people, the Church. Like the apostles, the bishops seek to extend the reign of Jesus Christ by establishing new local "churches" throughout the world.

SUMMARY AND CONCLUSION

The mission and ministry of Jesus Christ continues in the world through his body, his people, the Church. It is a great mystery why Jesus chose weak, sinful men like his apostles to carry out his divine mission. It is a mystery why Jesus *continues* to choose weak, sinful human beings—bishops, popes and *each* of us—to continue his mission in the world. Yet this is exactly what God has done.

We may be tempted, at times, to despair and give up on the Church Jesus founded, as we realize its weakness and the power of evil and Satan, who is still the greatest enemy of Christ and his Church. He "prowls around like a roaring lion, seeking some one to devour" (1 Peter 5:8).

However, there is no reason to despair. We are a people of hope, since God has won the definitive battle against evil, Satan and sin through Jesus' death on the cross. As Saint Paul wrote, "In all these things we are more than conquerors through him who loved us" (Romans 8:37). Jesus has conquered evil and given to his people, the Church, the final victory, which will be revealed when Jesus comes again in glory to judge the living and the dead. "This is the victory that overcomes the world, our faith" (1 John 5:4).

As we tell the story of God's new covenant people, the Church, we recognize times of failure and weakness. Still we see God's faithfulness and mercy as he continues to forgive, renew and restore the Church and raise it again and again from the pit of trouble and conflict to new heights of faith, charity and peace. Stories of great saints, those holy men and women who have advanced the kingdom of God by their sacrifice and faithfulness to Jesus Christ, constantly inspire us. This is *our* story of our lives and of our people. "Once you were no people but now you are God's people" (1 Peter 2:10). Let us thank the Lord for making us his people and for continuing to bless and strengthen our Church through his Holy Spirit.

the CHURCH *of the* APOSTLES *and the* FATHERS
(AD 50–600)

The Church of the apostles (the first-century Church) begins an era of the great early Christian leaders and theologians who are commonly known as the "Fathers of the Church." This period of the Church's life is often generally referred to as the patristic period or the period of the Fathers. An overview of important persons, events and movements during this period will show the development of the Catholic Church up to the seventh century.

THE FIRST CENTURY

Laying the Foundation

Much of what happened in Christianity in the first century is familiar to us from the New Testament. In the Acts of the Apostles, we read of the missionary expansion of the Church of Jesus Christ from its original home in Jerusalem, comprised of Jewish converts to Christ, to its extension to the gentiles in many parts of the Roman Empire until it finally reached Rome itself. The relative peace of this century, as well as the fine system of Roman roads and safe travel routes by sea, made the rapid expansion of Christianity possible. A common culture and language also aided this expansion. However, the real force behind the growth of Christianity was the Holy Spirit, who raised up a host of great apostles like Paul and martyrs like Stephen, the first martyr.

Christianity began as a seemingly insignificant offshoot of Judaism. In the first and early second centuries, most of its converts were from the lower social classes of Roman society, including numerous women, common people and slaves. At first the Roman government ignored these Christians, but in AD 64 Emperor Nero blamed them for a great fire in Rome that he himself had likely started. The apostles Peter and Paul, the leaders of the Church in Rome, were martyred in this short but bloody persecution. Christians buried their dead, prayed and sometimes hid in catacombs (underground burial vaults) of Rome during these early persecutions.

Why were Christians persecuted? Even the pagans recognized their mutual love and care for the poor, for widows and orphans, for victims of plague and famine and for those in prison and in the mines. "See how these Christians love one another"[1] was a common observation. Still, Christians were suspected as a secret society that met early on Sunday morning to eat the body and blood of a man, Christ, and perhaps to engage in sexual immorality, as many religious groups of the time did. Of course, these rumors were untrue, often based on a misunderstanding of what Christians did when they met on Sunday to pray, read the Hebrew Scriptures, share accounts of the life of Christ and letters from the apostles and celebrate the Lord's Supper, the Eucharist, as Jesus had commanded.

The Roman government began to suspect that Christians were enemies of the state, atheists who refused to worship the Roman gods or pay homage to the Roman emperor. The emperor Domitian launched a fierce persecution of Christians at the end of the first century because they refused to sacrifice to him as a god. In symbolic language the book of Revelation tells of this persecution by Rome (called Babylon).

The Christian writer Tertullian later observed, "The blood of the martyrs is the seed of the Church,"[2] and Christianity continued to grow by its witness of faith and courage. Christian bishops, the leaders of the Church after the death of the apostles, continued to be models of faith for God's people—such as the bishops of Rome after Peter: Linus, Anacletus and Clement. By the end of the first century, there were an estimated half-million Christians in the Roman Empire.

THE SECOND CENTURY

Continued Expansion and Defense of the Faith

Two model bishops who gave their lives for Christ at the beginning of the second century were Polycarp of Smyrna and Ignatius of Antioch. On his way to martyrdom in Rome about AD 110, Ignatius wrote seven letters—one to Polycarp and the others to Christian churches along the way—to encourage them in their faith. Ignatius even warned the Roman Christians not to attempt to prevent his death. He said that he wanted the lions to grind his flesh and bones like wheat so that he would become pure bread for Christ, like the bread of the Eucharist.

Martyrdom was considered a direct route to heaven, so martyrs were highly respected by the early Christians. In prayer they asked the martyrs to intercede before God's throne for the Church on earth (see Revelation 6:9–11; 7:9–17). There are important accounts of heroic women too, such as Saint Perpetua and Saint Felicity, who gave their lives for Christ.

In the second century the leadership structure of the Church took a definite form, which has remained unchanged in the Catholic Church to the present. Ignatius of Antioch reports as early as AD 110 that each local church was led by a single bishop. The bishop was assisted in his ministry by "presbyters" (later called "priests") who led the community in celebrating the Eucharist and administered other sacraments, as the local churches grew too large for the bishop to minister personally to everyone. The bishop was assisted by "deacons," who had the important role of serving the local church in practical ways, such as distributing money and goods to the poor and needy.

Guided by the Holy Spirit, the bishops began to work together in the second century to meet new challenges of the time and to develop common teaching. An example of common teaching was the formulation of creeds, short summaries of the Christian faith that were used to prepare candidates for baptism as well as to instruct all Christians in their faith.

The bishops also discussed what writings were to be considered God's inspired word for the whole Church. Some people, such as Marcion, had rejected the inspiration of the Hebrew Scriptures (our Old Testament) and accepted a very limited selection of Christian writings. Other groups, like the Gnostics, wanted to consider some very unusual writings as inspired by God. For example, one Gnostic gospel presents

Jesus as a little boy bringing clay birds to life and causing the death of some playmates who irritated him. In response to this the bishops began to develop official lists of inspired writings, called canons, which later resulted in a general agreement on what writings make up our Bible today. Even by the fourth century, however, the canon of the New Testament was not yet finalized. This shows the importance of the Holy Spirit's continual guiding of the bishops so that God's truth would come forth in all its fullness.

The bishops of the second century also had to meet the challenge of false teaching, such as the belief that God was only one person and consequently Jesus Christ was only a man (an "adopted son" but not God), or the opposite belief that Christians worshiped three gods instead of one. The Gnostics taught that Jesus was only divine, without a true human nature; he only appeared to be human (Docetism). All of these beliefs were condemned as false by the bishops.

The bishops corrected groups that split off from the Church for other reasons. Montanists, followers of a priest named Montanus, believed Jesus' Second Coming was going to be immediate. They wanted to impose a more rigorous standard of fasting on all Christians; they also considered their prophetic revelations equal in authority with the inspired writings of Paul and the four Gospels. When the Catholic bishops did not agree with this, the Montanists started their own church, which even attracted the brilliant North African defender of the Christian faith, Tertullian. The Montanists died out soon after Tertullian's death in AD 220.

Many other false teachings and splinter groups emerged in this century, but only the universal Church led by the united bishops endured. Often it was the bishop of Rome who provided the answer to a dispute. This led the famous defender of the faith Bishop Irenaeus of Lyons (in present-day France) to say of Rome: "Every other [local] church must be in harmony with this church [Rome] because of its outstanding pre-eminence."[3] In the middle of the third century, Bishop Cyprian of Carthage wrote: "To be in communion with the bishop of Rome is to be in communion with the Catholic Church."[4]

The persecution of Christians in the second century was sporadic, which allowed Christianity to spread even further and to make more converts from the upper classes of Roman society. God began to raise up intellectual leaders who could explain and defend the faith through reason and philosophy: Justin Martyr of the eastern Mediterranean region presented Christianity as "the true philosophy"; Irenaeus of Lyons saw all creation as being brought together and "summed up" in Christ; Athenagoras of Athens wrote an important defense of Christianity, and Clement of Alexandria founded the great school of Christian teaching for catechumens. Those "apologists" wrote to emperors to convince them not to persecute Christians, to Jews to convince them of the truth of Christianity and to groups of heretics who were destroying true Christianity (for example, the Gnostics who claimed to have a secret knowledge of the way of salvation not available to other Christians).

These Christian apologists demonstrated that Christianity was a reasonable and intellectually sound religion that could be understood and accepted by people of all cultures and lands. By the end of the second century, there were about two million Christians spread throughout the Roman Empire, in spite of the fact that it was still an illegal religion officially forbidden by the Roman state.

THE THIRD CENTURY

Persecution and Theological Development

The third century was primarily a time of expansion of Christianity as well as of organization and theological development. The relative peace for Christianity in the Roman Empire from AD 200 to 250 gave the Church time to evangelize and organize, and theologians time to think and write.

The first to organize Christian thought into a unified system, drawing heavily on Greek philosophy, was Origen of Alexandria (AD 184–254), who led the famous catechetical school there. In spite of some ideas that were later recognized as false (the devil could be saved, and souls are preexistent), Origen was the authority most quoted in the next century. Origen taught that Scripture was to be interpreted allegorically—presenting stories and images as symbols of deeper, spiritual truths.

The relative peace of the third century made many Christians grow comfortable and lax. The Church was shocked when Emperor Decius, fearing the growing numbers of Christians, called for the first empire-wide persecution of the Church in AD 250. Christians who refused to offer sacrifice to the Roman gods before special commissioners were imprisoned or put to death. Thousands of Christians renounced their faith ("apostatized") in the face of death, though some were martyred.

The persecution ended as suddenly as it had begun, in AD 251, and a dispute arose about whether those who had denied their Christian faith could be readmitted to the Church. Bishops Cornelius of Rome and Cyprian of Carthage taught that bishops could grant God's forgiveness even for serious sins, like apostasy, through prolonged, severe penances. Novatian, a presbyter of Rome, disagreed and founded his own church comprised only of people who had not denied their faith. The Catholic Church affirmed that God wanted his people to include repentant sinners and not just to comprise people who never sinned seriously.

This issue arose again after the persecution of Emperor Diocletian from AD 303 to 311, in which bishops and priests were compelled by the government to surrender Bibles, liturgical books and sacred vessels used at Mass. After the persecution ended, a group of Christians in North Africa refused to recognize the authority of those priests and bishops who had fled the persecution or who had turned over the sacred books and vessels, even after they had repented. This group started their own church, named the Donatist Church after one of their bishops, Donatus. The Donatists only recognized the authority of leaders who had refused to surrender their sacred objects. Again, the Catholic Church maintained that even those leaders who had failed "under fire" could continue to lead because their authority came from Christ himself. Even their personal sin and weakness could not remove the commission and grace given them through the sacrament of holy orders.

An important principle of Catholic life emerges from this: The authority to confer a sacrament, to teach or to lead in the Church does not depend on the worthiness or personal holiness of the ordained minister. Jesus continues to work through and to forgive weak human vessels, to show that the power in the sacraments and the ordained ministry comes from God, not man. Perhaps the best image of the Church in the third century was that of Saint Cyprian, who wrote of it as a great ark or ship, which holds sinners as well as saints and martyrs and yet is the only place where salvation can be found in a world bound by sin.

THE FOURTH CENTURY

The Christian Empire and the Arian Crisis

In spite of the vigorous persecution of the Roman emperors Decius and Diocletian, the number of Christians swelled to about five million by AD 300, out of a total population of fifty million in the Roman Empire. In AD 311 Emperor Galerius ended the long persecution that had begun in AD 302 with Diocletian. However, an event the following year (AD 312) changed the destiny of the Catholic Church and of all Western civilization.

The Roman emperor of the West (western Mediterranean region), Constantine, had a vision, a religious experience that assured him that he would conquer through the Greek monogram of Christ, the *Chi-Rho.* When he marked the shields of his soldiers with this sign and won a major victory at the Battle of the Milvian Bridge near Rome, he attributed his victory to the Christian God. The next year (AD 313), he passed the Edict of Milan with the agreement of the emperor of the East, Licinius, thus granting religious toleration throughout the Roman Empire. Christianity was no longer an illegal religion!

That was only the first step. Constantine began to actively support Christianity, seeing it as the new unifying force within the Roman Empire, replacing the Roman gods. Constantine built churches; passed laws honoring Sunday, Christmas and other Christian holy days; protected Christian clergy and more.

Despite disputes over the depth or motivation of Constantine's conversion to Christianity, he professed to be a Christian from AD 313 onward and was baptized on his deathbed in AD 337.

Christians throughout the empire rejoiced at the conversion of Constantine. Here is what the Church had been praying for and awaiting for centuries—a Christian emperor! Yet the Church was soon to find that this was not a pure, unmixed blessing. The alliance of the Church and the state created many tensions, as the history of the fourth century shows.

An example is the story of the Arian crisis, the greatest challenge to confront the Church up to that time and perhaps in the whole of the Church's history. A priest named Arius, of Alexandria, Egypt, began teaching that the Son of God (manifested in Jesus Christ) was not God but the highest creature of God. He supported his argument with a number of Bible texts (see Matthew 27:46; Mark 13:32; 15:34; John 14:28), especially those that emphasized Jesus' human nature. Surprisingly, Arius convinced a number of Catholic bishops that he was right.

When the bishops began to argue among themselves about Arius's teaching, Constantine saw this as a threat to the unity of the empire and decided to intervene. He called all the bishops together for the first "ecumenical" or worldwide council (meeting) of bishops at Nicaea (in Turkey) in AD 325. The bishops decided Arius was wrong and developed a creed to clarify the Church's belief. This creed used the Greek word *homoousios* to refute Arius—saying that Jesus was "of the same substance" or "one in being" with the Father. In other words, whatever the Father is, so is the Son; if the Father is God, so is the Son. Arius's position that the Son was not God but a creature was condemned.

The dispute should have ended there, but it did not. Two or three bishops later decided that the Church could not settle this question by using an unbiblical word *(homoousios)* and decided that Arius was actually right. They managed to change the minds of a few other bishops and then approached the emperor Constantine to convince him.

Here begins an unfortunate chapter of the involvement of the Church with the Roman state. When the pro-Arian bishops swayed the emperor and succeeding emperors to their opinion, the emperors began to put political pressure on the bishops supporting the Council of Nicaea's creed. In fact, a number of pro-Nicene bishops were expelled from their local dioceses by force.

To summarize, three things resulted from this crisis:

1. The realization that it is dangerous to the Church for secular rulers to become involved with resolving theological and doctrinal disputes and with Church affairs in general.

2. The emergence of some great, heroic figures who stubbornly defended the truth that the Son is truly God. The greatest of these was Saint Athanasius, bishop of Alexandria, exiled five times by pro-Arian emperors for defending the Council of Nicaea. He always returned to defend the faith, and he died in Alexandria.

3. The Catholic principle that it is legitimate to use nonbiblical words to define or clarify a truth of faith, if necessary. Catholics believe that the Holy Spirit is not limited to the Bible in guiding the Church. God's truth is conveyed through authentic Christian tradition—through creeds as well as through the Bible. The term *homoousios*

was the only term that could be used to adequately refute Arius and to affirm the Christian belief in the full divinity of Jesus Christ, the Son of God.

At times during this crisis, things looked bleak for the cause of the Council of Nicaea. In AD 361 Saint Jerome wrote, "The entire world groaned and was astonished to find itself Arian."[5]

Soon after this the tide began to turn. Following the tireless work of Athanasius in Egypt, three great theologians from Cappadocia in Asia Minor emerged to defend the Nicene Creed: Saints Basil of Caesarea, Gregory of Nyssa and Gregory of Nazianzen. Their writings and influence convinced bishops who were still neutral or unsure to support the Nicene position.

In AD 381, the Council of Constantinople reaffirmed that the Son is "one in being" *(homoousios)* with the Father and added that the Holy Spirit is also fully God, as the Cappadocian Fathers had argued. The Nicene Creed that Catholics say at Sunday Mass today is actually the profession of faith confirmed by the bishops at this council of AD 381. Unfortunately, the Arian beliefs had already spread to some tribes surrounding the Roman Empire (the Visigoths, Ostrogoths and Vandals), who made trouble for the Catholic Church in the next century when they took over large segments of the Roman Empire.

One result of the end of the persecution of Christians in the Roman Empire was the end of martyrdom as a witness to the faith. In the fourth century there emerged some new heroes of the Christian faith: the hermits, or monks, also known as the Desert Fathers. These men and women responded literally to Jesus' call to sell everything, give to the poor and follow him.

In order to follow Christ through a life of penance and prayer, they went out into the desert or wilderness to live a life alone with God. The word *monk* comes from the Latin word for "alone" *(monos)*.

Antony, an Egyptian peasant, fled alone into the desert around AD 270 and emerged in AD 305 as a great spiritual master. Saint Athanasius immortalized Antony and helped spread the "monastic" or "ascetic" movement by writing Antony's biography. Athanasius remained a great friend and supporter of the monks throughout his life.

Pachomius, another Egyptian, founded a community of ascetics in the desert near the Nile River which gave birth to new monastic ways of life. Most monks after this either lived near each other in loosely knit villages or joined to live a life with certain common times of prayer, worship and labor. They spent most of their time in prayer, some in work and usually always in silence.

This new Christian way of life, the monastic or ascetic movement, was not just a fad or passing fancy. It spread rapidly throughout the Roman Empire and attracted many who desired to follow Jesus Christ and lead a life of prayer and self-denial in a radical way. Even though today some people might consider this a strange way of life or an escape from reality, it witnessed to people of that time and continues to do so today. Monasticism testifies that Christians are not to live for success and pleasure in this world but are here to worship God (which was the main work of the monks) and to prepare for the life of the world to come. The monks were admired by other Christians of the time as the new martyrs, the new radical witnesses for Christ.

Even though the monks had fled to the desert to escape worldliness, some of them were called back into the active life to serve as bishops, leaders of the Church. The Cappadocian Fathers (Basil and the two Gregorys) started as monks and then were chosen to become bishops because of their holiness and gifts of leadership. In fact, Saint Basil of Caesarea wrote the first great "rule," or way of life, for monks in Eastern Christianity. Many of the great bishops of the East, and popes and bishops of Western (Latin-speaking) Christianity in the next few centuries, began as monks. Saint John Chrysostom (AD 354–407), the famous "golden-mouthed" speaker who was bishop of Constantinople until he was exiled by the emperor, began as a monk.

Saint Martin of Tours founded a monastery in Gaul (France) in AD 371 and is often called the Father of Western Monasticism. The two greatest Latin-speaking fathers of the Western Church in the fourth century, Saint Augustine and Saint Jerome, lived as monks, at least for a time. Saint Jerome, who was the great Bible scholar of the Latin-speaking world, spent much of his life as an ascetic in a cave in Bethlehem.

Saint Augustine lived a monastic life with some friends after his conversion to Christianity. He was converted through the prayers of his mother, Monica, and the preaching of Saint Ambrose, bishop of Milan. Even after he was made bishop of the North African city of Hippo, Augustine developed a rule of life for his clergy with whom he lived. This disciplined way of life enabled Augustine, by the power of God, to become one of the most productive and influential writers in Christian history. He wrote his *Confessions*, commentaries on Scripture, works against both the Donatist Church and a heresy called

Pelagianism, great theological treatises (such as *On the Trinity*) and finally his magnificent statement of the relationship between the Church and the world, *The City of God*.

The fourth century was one of crisis and of greatness for the Catholic Church. In AD 381 Theodosius declared Christianity the *only* official religion of the Roman Empire and moved to end paganism. The numbers of Christians soared and led to the problem of many people joining the Church for political expedience. It was now easier and more comfortable to be a Christian than a pagan or a follower of any other religion.

This created new challenges for the Church. A system of Christian initiation, teaching large numbers of new converts, was developed by bishops such as Cyril of Jerusalem. Sunday sermons were very long, sometimes three to four hours, to instruct this influx of new Christians.

The pope, the bishop of Rome, was given full authority over all churches of the West by the Council of Sardica in AD 343, which was confirmed by Emperor Gratian in AD 378. Pope Damasus (pope from AD 366 to 384) declared that the authority of the pope ultimately came not from a council or an emperor but from the Lord himself through his commission to Peter (see Matthew 16:18). Saint Ambrose agreed that "where Peter is, there is the Church," in support of the pope's authority.[6] Saint Jerome wrote to Pope Damasus: "I follow no one as leader except Christ alone, and therefore I want to remain in union in the Church with you, that is, with the chair [office] of Peter. I know that on this rock the Church is founded."[7]

Even though the bishops of Constantinople gained increased authority in this century as "patriarchs" (or chief bishops) of the Eastern or Greek-speaking churches, no decision could be binding on all of the Catholic Church without the approval of the bishop of Rome. As we shall see, the courage and authority of the pope and of all the bishops was to be severely tested in the fifth century both by theological disputes and by the takeover of the Roman Empire by invading peoples.

THE FIFTH CENTURY

Questions of Belief and New Political Alignments

The fifth century began with a definite political division between Eastern (Greek-speaking) and Western (Latin-speaking) empires. We can almost recount their histories as separate stories.

The sack of Rome in AD 410 by the Visigoth tribes under Alaric shook the Latin West. Gradually different tribes, such as the Vandals and Huns, conquered parts of the Western Empire, until the West was entirely under the control of these tribes by AD 476. As the political power of Rome disintegrated, the pope and the other bishops began to lead and defend God's people physically as well as spiritually. Probably the most courageous leader was Pope Leo I, pope from AD 440 to 461, who dissuaded Attila the Hun from attacking Rome and persuaded Geneseric the Vandal to plunder Rome without destroying it.

The "good news" is that by the sixth and seventh centuries, Catholic Christians would manage to convert many of these peoples, some of whom were Arians, to orthodox Catholic Christianity. The Church often "conquers her conquerors" in this way—through conversion to Christ and his Church.

The greatest theological challenge to the Church in the West, after the Donatist conflict was put to rest by political force in AD 412, was the influence of Pelagianism. Pelagius was a British monk who denied that human nature was corrupted by original sin. Thus man did not need God's grace to avoid sin but only good examples of moral living, like Jesus.

The Western Church came to realize that Pelagius was wrong because he made salvation primarily dependent on human effort instead of God's grace. Some theologians thought that Saint Augustine went too far in the other direction in refuting Pelagius, making everything depend on God's grace and very little on human cooperation with God. The Second Council of Orange in AD 529 approved a modified version of Saint Augustine's view, emphasizing an absolute need for God's grace to do anything good but also recognizing the necessity of human cooperation to accept God's grace.

In the Eastern Empire the political situation was more stable, which gave bishops and theologians a chance to focus on some theological questions. First, the bishop of Constantinople, Nestorius, denied that Mary could be called *Theotokos*, meaning "God-bearer" or Mother of God. He was part of a theological group called the school of Antioch, which did not want to risk any confusion between the divine and human. They believed that calling Mary the Mother of God threatened to mix up God and man, since Mary did not bring God into existence. However, another noted group, called the school of Alexandria, led by the bishop of Alexandria, Cyril, saw no problem in calling Mary the Mother of God, since this way of speaking safeguarded the *unity* of Jesus' human and divine nature.

The issue was settled in AD 431 by the Council of Ephesus, an ecumenical council of Catholic bishops, which declared

Nestorius wrong and affirmed the long-standing tradition of Christian prayer in which Mary was honored as Mother of God. We understand this to mean that Mary is mother of God *in his human nature*, the mother of "God made man," and *not* the mother of Jesus' divine nature. Mary is the mother of a *person*, Jesus Christ, who is both fully God and fully man.

This initial dispute concerning the natures of Christ gave rise to another controversy in the middle of the century. Without examining the political rivalry behind the scenes between the patriarch of Constantinople and the patriarch of Alexandria, there was a serious theological debate about whether Jesus possessed one nature as a person—the divine nature—or two distinct natures, divine and human. The resolution finally came at the Council of Chalcedon in AD 451, which brought together and balanced the legitimate beliefs about Christ from the school of Antioch and the school of Alexandria. The council declared that Jesus exists *in two natures*, the divine and the human, which come together "without confusion or change, without division or separation" to form the *one undivided person* of Jesus Christ, the Son of God incarnate.

A key to the resolution of this dispute was a timely letter of Pope Leo I, which anticipated and guided the final agreement of the Eastern bishops at the Council of Chalcedon. This council remains a foundation of our understanding of the person of Jesus Christ even today.

Unfortunately, the story doesn't end here. As happened after the Council of Nicaea in AD 325, some Christians in the East rejected the agreement of the Council of Chalcedon and continued to believe that Jesus Christ possessed only one *(mono)* nature *(physis)*, the divine nature. These people referred to themselves as Monophysites and started their own churches in the Eastern part of the empire, which exist even to this day. Some (even most) of the best theologians in the East in the fifth and sixth centuries were Monophysites. Even the political maneuvering of the Eastern emperors like Justinian failed to destroy or to win over the Monophysites.

The Eastern Empire showed great development of theological thought and ideas in the fifth and sixth centuries. This so-called Byzantine theology was enriched by Greek philosophical thought, including the logic of Aristotle. Byzantine theology not only quoted the Bible but also began to use quotations from the Greek Fathers of the Church, up to Cyril of Alexandria, as authoritative sources.

In the East there was no great gulf between clergy and laity or Church and state. Emperors such as Justinian considered themselves theologians and felt a responsibility for guiding the Church, even to the extent of nominating and deposing bishops. This union of spiritual and temporal authority in the person of the emperor, which arose in the Eastern segment of the Church, is known as "Caesaropapism." There was a close alliance between the Church and the state in the East at this time, which continued until the Islamic conquest.

The Eastern (Byzantine) Christians also developed a rich and meaningful way of worship, which endures even today. They emphasize the holiness of the divine mysteries of faith and are dramatic and splendid in their liturgical celebration and ceremonies. They developed their own liturgies, such as the Liturgy of Saint John Chrysostom, which grew increasingly distinct from Western, Latin liturgies. The Eastern Church also stressed veneration of Mary, the saints and relics.

THE SIXTH CENTURY

The End of One Era and the Beginning of a New Era

The great period of theological and spiritual learning called the Age of the Fathers of the Church began to draw to a close in the sixth century. The West was already primarily preoccupied with survival in the face of invading tribes from the north, east and south.

Then came a strange turn of events. The Eastern Empire, which had been relatively secure, began to be threatened by the advance of Islam, which eventually overwhelmed it. The Western Empire, under the control of warlike, non-Christian tribes, began to convert these peoples to Christianity, and one by one their kingdoms in the West collapsed (Burgundians in AD 532; Vandals in AD 533; Ostrogoths in AD 553). Meanwhile, Clovis, king of the Franks, was converted to Christianity in AD 496 and became a great support to the Church.

Saint Benedict founded a monastic community at Monte Cassino in Italy in AD 529, which would soon change the face of Europe. Based on a sane policy of "work and pray" and of monks' staying in one place, the monasteries of Saint Benedict became places where Roman and Western culture was preserved and where the gospel was spread. Under Pope Gregory I (the Great), the Benedictines became a great missionary force. To quote author Alfred Lapple:

> *The achievements of the Benedictine monks can be summarized by three symbols: the Cross (they were messengers of the Christian faith), the book (pioneers and preservers of Western culture), and the plow (promoters of civilization*

and new settlements). According to the English historian Edward Gibbon, "A single Benedictine monastery may have done more for the cause of knowledge than Oxford and Cambridge combined." [8]

Even before the Benedictines, though, Saint Patrick had brought the gospel to Ireland (AD 461) and founded austere monasteries much like the early monasteries of Saint Pachomius in Egypt. Saint Columba, an Irish monk, planted a Celtic monastery at Iona in Scotland in AD 563. So the conversion of the British Isles was underway. The Middle Ages of Church life had begun.

the CHURCH *of the* MIDDLE AGES
(AD 600–1300)

The next seven hundred years of the history of Christianity were marked by the conversion of new peoples and tribes to Jesus Christ. It was a time of political turmoil and warfare, which often involved the struggle to determine the proper relationship of the Catholic Church to the state. In the West this led to the emergence of "Christendom," the alliance of Church and state.

Christendom bore much good fruit but also resulted in continual tension between the popes and emperors and between other leaders of Church and state. There was also increasing tension between the Roman Catholic Church of the West and the Holy Orthodox Church of the East. Serious heresies and distortions of true Christian teaching appeared.

There were also many tremendous advances in Christianity in the Middle Ages. Some of the greatest Christian saints and scholars emerged, and the culture of Christianity reached new heights in art, literature, architecture and theology. New religious orders flourished, bringing new life to the Church, and old monastic orders were renewed. At times Christianity seemed to be on the verge of collapse in this period, but the grace of God proved to be more powerful than any situation, bringing the Church through many perils and blessing it with growth and victory. Political forces prevented this from being a period of missionary expansion beyond the boundaries of Europe and Byzantium (the eastern Mediterranean area), but it was a time of the establishment of Europe as a Christian continent and of the preservation of the Christian faith in the East in the face of the spread of Islam.

THE SEVENTH CENTURY

The collapse of the old Roman Empire did not discourage Saint Gregory the Great, pope from AD 590 to 604, who laid the foundation for the Church in Western Europe in the Middle Ages. When secular rulers failed, Pope Gregory took control of central Italy and saved Rome many times from plunder by the Lombards. He sent delegates to the churches in the West to encourage them and strengthen their allegiance to the pope. His theological and spiritual writings shaped the thought of the Middle Ages.

Pope Gregory I personally sent a Benedictine monk, Augustine, to convert the Angles and Saxons in England. Soon afterward King Aethelbert of Kent was baptized, and Augustine was named first bishop of Canterbury. The Irish or Celtic monks, led by Saint Aidan and Saint Cuthbert, assisted in the conversion of England, which soon became a Christian nation. The *History of the English Church and People* by Saint Bede, a Benedictine monk, tells the story of England's conversion and the spread of Christianity. Soon England was sending missionaries to Europe, such as the Benedictine monk Willibrord, who became known as the Apostle to the Netherlands and was made the bishop of that territory in AD 695.

In Eastern Christianity the Sixth Ecumenical Council of bishops was held in Constantinople in AD 680–681 (the Third Council of Constantinople). The bishops condemned the belief that Jesus had only one will, the divine will—a heresy called Monotheletism. If Jesus had both a divine and human nature, he had to have both a divine and human will.

Politically Islam was a dark cloud on the horizon. Mohammed had died in AD 632, his followers were growing in military power, and they threatened to invade Europe. Only their defeats by the Eastern Christian forces at Constantinople in AD 674–678, and again in AD 717–718, and by Charles Martel, father of Pepin, at the Battle of Tours in AD 732, prevented Europe from being conquered by the forces of Islam.

THE EIGHTH CENTURY

The conversion of the tribes of Europe continued in the eighth century under the leadership of the English Benedictine monk Winfrid, better known as Saint Boniface, the Apostle of Germany; he evangelized from AD 723 to 739. There is a well-known story that when Boniface cut down a tree the people thought to be sacred, the Oak of Thor, in order to use the wood for building a church, everyone converted to Christianity because Boniface wasn't struck dead by the gods. Boniface was only one example of hundreds of Benedictine monks who worked and died to establish the Catholic faith in Europe under the direction of the pope.

With the help of Boniface, the pope formed an alliance with the kings of the Franks in Gaul (now France), beginning with King Pepin (or Pippin). In AD 754 Pope Stephen II anointed Pepin king and honored him with the title Patrician of the Romans, a title originally reserved for the Roman emperors. This created a bond of loyalty between the pope and the Frankish kings, which reached its summit with the coronation of Charles (the Great, also called Charlemagne), son of Pepin, in Rome in AD 800.

The relationship between the popes and Charles, who ruled from AD 768 to 814, developed over many years. The unfortunate effect of this alliance was that it alienated the Eastern Christian Church, which maintained loyalty to the Byzantine emperor in Constantinople, whom they saw as the true Roman emperor.

Charles the Great did not help the relationship between the Western and Eastern Churches when he disagreed with the decision of the Second Council of Nicaea in the East (AD 787), fought to capture territory claimed by the Byzantine emperor and wanted to compel the Eastern Church to add a new phrase, *filioque*, to the Nicene Creed. The Creed originally stated that the Holy Spirit proceeds *from the Father* (see John 15:26); the Western version that Charles advocated (based on the theology of Saint Augustine) says that the Holy Spirit proceeds from the Father *and the Son (filioque)*. This situation illustrates the problem of the close alliance between the Church and the state. Charles the Great was a great defender and promoter of the Christian faith and the Catholic Church; however, he also wanted to control the Church and make theological decisions.

At one point Charles wrote the pope and told him that it was the pope's job to pray for the Church but his job, as emperor, to rule it. In theory there was a division between worldly (temporal) and spiritual authority in this alliance between Church and state; in practice, however, a strong emperor or king would always take control of some spiritual affairs, and a strong pope would take control of worldly or political affairs. Sometimes kings and other secular rulers even claimed the right to select and install priests and bishops without consulting the pope or other bishops. This practice, called lay investiture, became one of the most disputed issues between the popes and secular rulers in the Middle Ages. Part of the price of the security of having a Christian king or emperor was his involvement, or interference, in Church or spiritual affairs.

Charles the Great's method of evangelizing people to Christianity was to conquer a territory and then give the conquered people a choice to be baptized either "with water or with blood." This was a harsh age when the mass of people were illiterate and simply followed the religion of their ruler. Catholicism became more of a cultural religion, in which people were baptized *en masse* with the hope that they could be instructed in the Christian faith later. The Church feared a relapse into paganism.

The hope for preserving civilization and instructing the ignorant in their faith lay with the monasteries. Even Charles the Great attempted to revive learning by gathering a community of scholars in his own palace—led by the learned English monk Alcuin (his secretary)—and by dictating that every bishop should establish a school at his cathedral church. This made some impact, but after Charles died and the Carolingian Empire was divided, the light of learning waned. Except for the monasteries, Europe sank into a time of intellectual and spiritual darkness.

The Eastern Christians battling the forces of Islam also experienced a theological crisis in the eighth century. In AD 730 Byzantine Emperor Leo III published a decree forbidding Christians to venerate icons, beautiful painted images of Christ or the saints (iconoclasm). Although this had become an important part of the spiritual life and devotion of Eastern Christians, Leo III felt that this "worship of images" was forbidden by the Bible and so ordered the destruction of all icons.

Pope Gregory III and many Eastern Christians protested this, but it was not until the Empress Irene called the Second Council of Nicaea (the Seventh Ecumenical Council) in AD 787 that the veneration of icons was approved once again. That council distinguished between the *veneration* given to icons because they are images of God or holy persons and *adoration*, which is due to God alone. The Roman Catholic Church has always agreed with this, having consistently made use of pictures, mosaics, stained-glass windows, statues and paintings on walls of churches to teach and remind people of the truths of their faith. Pope Gregory the Great taught that pictures are the books of laypeople, since most people of that time were illiterate.[1]

THE NINTH CENTURY

The beginning of the ninth century appeared promising for the Western Catholic Church. Charles the Great imposed the Christian faith on his captive subjects in northern and central Europe, and gradually the people embraced Christianity and rejected the worst abuses of their pagan past. The popes grew more influential too, and after Charles's death, his son, Louis the Pious, announced that the authority of his office was dependent upon the pope. Louis's son, Lothar, was crowned in Rome in AD 823, and after that all the rulers of the Holy Roman Empire were crowned in Rome. Pope Nicholas I (AD 858–867), the strongest pope of the century, taught that the emperor's duty was to protect the Roman Catholic Church but not to govern it.

Unfortunately, the power of the emperor was weakened by internal difficulties and by invasions of the Vikings from the north and Hungarians and Muslim Saracens from the east and south. The unity and peace of the great empire forged by Charles the Great began to fall apart, and Europe was plunged into an age of feudalism—splitting of the continent into small divisions struggling for survival and battling each other.

Accompanying the decline of the Western Empire was a decline of the Western Church. After Nicholas I there were no popes who could effectively lead the Church in this situation. There was even a brief schism, or breaking of relationship, between the popes and the patriarchs of Constantinople between AD 858 and 879. The division arose over some territorial ambitions of Pope Nicholas I and resulted in the allegation by Patriarch Photius that the Roman Catholic Church was unorthodox for using *filioque* in the Creed, upholding the doctrine of purgatory and other alleged errors.

Fortunately, Photius retracted his charges; he and the new pope were reconciled, and there was relative peace between the Eastern and Western Churches in the tenth century. However, the basic issues were never resolved, and the tragic schism between East and West beginning in 1054 was the sad consequence of this.

As the ninth century ended, Islam was suppressing the Church in the East, and political instability and weak popes stifled the Western Church. Clergy were controlled by secular rulers and lapsed into illiteracy and unfaithfulness to their vow of celibacy. Even most of the monasteries had lost their fervor and become worldly or corrupt. The decline of the Western society and the decline of the Church went hand in hand, since the two were interrelated in so many ways.

Yet even in times of weakness, God continued to work through the Church. Toward the end of the ninth century, two monks, Methodius and Cyril, began a mission to the Khazars and the Slavic people in Eastern Europe. Not only did they bring the Christian faith to a new people but also Cyril invented the Slavonic (Cyrillic) alphabet, which provided the Slavs with a new language and a vehicle for their culture.

THE TENTH CENTURY

It is an unfortunate fact that sometimes the spiritual condition of the Church of Christ is no better than the spiritual condition of the society as a whole. This was true of the tenth century. In its first sixty years, the office of pope was controlled by Roman aristocrats who were unworthy of their high office. The worst of them, Pope John XII (AD 955–964), was so corrupt that God delivered the Catholic Church from him through a secular ruler, Otto I (the Great), the first Holy Roman Emperor of the German nation. Otto had Pope John XII crown him and then deposed him.

Otto and his successors wanted to use the Catholic Church as an instrument to help restore order in the empire.

Lay investiture, the selection by the emperors of bishops and even popes, was one of their primary ways to control the Church. By God's mercy the popes nominated by the German emperors during this period were of high quality, especially Pope Sylvester II (AD 999–1003). As a result the Western Church began to revive.

Another key to the renewal of the Church at this time was the renewal of monastic life, which began with the founding of a new monastery, Cluny, in France in AD 910. This Benedictine monastery set aside certain monks for full-time prayer, and silence was observed by all, except when chanting the Divine Office. The monks elected their own abbot and were answerable to the pope alone, so there was no lay control.

The monastery was so effective that many bishops and princes invited Cluny to form daughter houses in their dioceses (in the Netherlands, Italy, Spain, England and Germany). The first monastic order had begun, which embraced fifteen hundred houses by 1100. The reform of Cluny led to the renewal of other monasteries and to the founding of new monastic orders, such as the Camaldolese by Saint Romuald and the Carthusians by Saint Bruno.

This fire of holiness began to renew the Catholic Church in the eleventh century, as many monks were called from their monasteries to become bishops in dioceses that were open to reform. The Cluny houses, which were directed by the pope himself, became a way for the pope to regain spiritual and moral authority. The great popes of the next two centuries— Gregory VII, Urban II and Paschal II—were originally monks of the Cluniac order.

THE ELEVENTH CENTURY

The new millennium began auspiciously with King (Saint) Stephen being crowned king of Hungary in AD 1000, seeing himself as a servant of Christ and his Church. The German emperors of the Ottonian Empire continued to control the Western Church in the eleventh century, but their nomination of able popes and their support of the Church had one unanticipated effect. Popes and cardinals began to realize that ownership of land and selection of bishops and popes by emperors and secular rulers were infringements on the freedom of the Church. They believed that even emperors were subject to the spiritual authority of the Catholic hierarchy.

This was fine in theory, but no pope was bold and strong enough to put it into practice until the election of Cardinal Hildebrand as Pope Gregory VII in 1073. With the fiery temperament and conviction of an Old Testament prophet, Gregory declared (in his famous *Dictatus Papae*, 1075) that the pope had been given supreme authority by Christ through Peter. The pope had universal authority in the Church and also the right to depose emperors or to change laws that conflicted with either God's law or Church authority. Most of all Gregory used his authority to reform the Catholic Church, which was in dire need of reform on all levels.

Gregory VII demonstrated that with God's help the Catholic Church *could* be renewed through a pope. He began by insisting that the priests be faithful to their vow of celibacy and reject all forms of simony (accepting money for spiritual services). When secular rulers or bishops were hesitant to enforce this decree because of their own self-interests, Gregory sent out his own legates throughout the empire, with documents of excommunication for anyone who refused to reform.

Gregory's power was best shown when he excommunicated the Holy Roman Emperor Henry IV for failing to support the reform of the Church. Henry came on his knees in the snow at Canossa to seek the pope's forgiveness, which was granted. Henry IV, however, shrewdly used the papal pardon to regain his political power and then launched a military campaign against the Papal States. Though Henry was repelled by the Normans, Pope Gregory was exiled from Rome and died in 1085. From his exile Gregory wrote: "Since the day when the Church placed me on its apostolic throne, my whole desire and the end of all my striving has been that the Holy Church...should recover her honor and remain free and chaste and Catholic."[2]

Gregory VII's work, supported by the monasteries, did greatly advance the cause of the reform of the Catholic Church and secured its freedom from control of civil rulers who wanted to use the Church for their own purposes. His theory of the authority of the pope was nothing new, but it bolstered and brought into practice what the Catholic Church had believed for centuries about the pope's role of leadership in the Church and the world.

The following popes of the tenth century, Urban II (1088–1099) and Paschal II (1099–1118), were also strong, holy men who continued the work of renewal and reform. Pope Urban II strengthened the papal role of leadership by calling for the First Crusade at the Council of Clermont in 1095, as an attempt to free the holy places of the East from Muslim control. Urban certainly did not envision the Crusades' turning out as they did but saw them as a practical means for Western Catholics to express their faith in Christ's lordship in the world and to assist the Christians of the East, who had suffered long under Islamic rule.

The eleventh century marks one of the saddest moments of the history of the Church, the schism between the Church of the East and the Church of the West in 1054. This division certainly violates the will of God, who sent Jesus to form one people, one Church. At this time Christianity became divided into the Catholic Church, recognizing the pope as its earthly head, and the Orthodox Church, led by its patriarchs, such as the patriarch of Constantinople.

What caused this schism? The events immediately surrounding it are only symptoms of difficulties that had been brewing for centuries. Most historians would say that the split between East and West was both ecclesial (dealing with the primacy of the pope) and theological (dealing with the *filioque* and other issues). Within ecumenical dialogue these are still the two major barriers to unity today.

Concerning the primacy of the pope, the central question is whether the pope has universal governing and teaching authority in the whole Church. The West believes that he does; the East believes that all the patriarchs, including the bishop of Rome, are equal in authority.

In 1054 the patriarch of Constantinople, Michael Caerularius, criticized certain Western Church practices, addressed the pope as "brother" instead of "father" and refused for three months to see the pope's legates who had come to Constantinople. These legates finally left a Bull of Excommunication on the altar of the patriarch's church and left Constantinople "shaking the dust from their feet" (see Matthew 10:14). A few days later Michael Caerularius responded by excommunicating the papal legates and the pope. These mutual excommunications were not lifted until 1965, when Pope Paul VI and Patriarch Athenagoras met, warmly embraced and removed them. By God's grace the work of reunifying the Eastern Orthodox Church and the Roman Catholic Church is now fully underway.

Despite the Church's failings, the gospel of Jesus Christ continued to be spread. Denmark and Norway were converted to Christianity in the eleventh century, followed shortly afterward by Sweden (1164). Russia had received missionaries from both the East and West, until the Russian prince decided to accept baptism in the Byzantine Church, which later became the Russian Orthodox Church, with its own patriarch in Moscow.

THE TWELFTH CENTURY

Because so many themes emerge in this century, they are more clearly grasped when divided into topics:

1. *Church-state Relations in the West.*

The pope and the Holy Roman Emperor continued to struggle over who had the right to select bishops and abbots, until finally a compromise was reached: the Concordat of Worms in 1122. This decreed that bishops and abbots would be elected by the laws of the Church, with the civil ruler investing them with civil authority if he wished, and the Church endowing them with their ring and bishop's staff and consecrating them for their spiritual office. Thus the pope, abbots and bishops were caught up into two worlds, the world of political power and the world of spiritual leadership.

The popes of the twelfth and thirteenth centuries were constantly aligning themselves with different rulers and nations to preserve the freedom of the papal states and to maintain a balance of power among the states of Europe that would prevent any one ruler from controlling the Church. Sometimes the popes failed. The Emperor Frederick I (Barbarossa), first of the Hohenstaufen family to rule as Holy Roman Emperor, seized Rome in 1159 and forced Pope Alexander III to flee. Alexander then allied himself with the Lombard League in northern Italy, defeated Frederick's army at Legnano in 1176 and made peace with Frederick. Reconciled with the Church, Frederick led the Third Crusade after the fall of Jerusalem in 1187.

In England Archbishop Thomas à Becket of Canterbury stood up for the rights and liberties of the Church until the Norman king, Henry II, forced Thomas to flee to France for six years. Because of Thomas's popularity with the people, the king allowed him to return in 1170. When Henry threw a fit of rage because of Thomas's continued support of papal policy in England, some of Henry's soldiers murdered Thomas on the steps of the altar of his cathedral in Canterbury. This atrocity shocked all of Europe. The pope excommunicated Henry, who did penance and revoked his claims against the Church. Thomas à Becket was canonized a saint in 1173 after many miracles at his tomb were verified.

2. *The Crusades.*

All these political struggles were seen by the popes as necessary to maintain the freedom of the Church from the manipulation and domination of secular rulers. The use of armies and military alliances by the popes was justified as self-defense—defending the papal territories and the right of the pope to govern the Church freely.

The Crusades, though, were a different case. The Crusades were military expeditions organized by the Church for the liberation of the Holy Land from Muslim control and for the defense of the Christian faith and protection of Christian pilgrims. Saint Augustine had developed the idea of "just war," and the Church believed that the Crusades were in this category. In fact, those who participated in the Crusades were granted by the Church full remission of all punishment due to their sins. Urban II, who called for the First Crusade, forbade any unworthy motive for going on a Crusade, such as for glory or temporal gain.

In theory the Crusades may have been justified, but due to man's fallen nature, the results of these wars were often tragic. The First Crusade was a military success, but the expulsion of the Greek patriarch in Antioch deepened the schism between the Eastern Church and Rome, and the Crusaders indiscriminately murdered hundreds of innocent people when they captured Jerusalem.

Even though the saintly Bernard of Clairvaux preached in support of the Second Crusade in 1146, it was a military failure. The Third Crusade in 1189 intended to recapture Jerusalem from Saladin the Turk, but all that was accomplished was a treaty guaranteeing the safety of Christian pilgrims in the Holy Land. Most would agree that these Crusades fell short of their intended goals and even weakened the relations between

Eastern and Western Christianity, as the leaders of the later Crusades increasingly went crusading for unholy motives.

3. *Church Reform and Early Heresies.*

The reform movement within the Catholic Church that began in the eleventh century continued into the twelfth. Robert of Molesme founded a monastery at Citeaux in 1098, which was the beginning of the new Cistercian Order. One of the dynamic young monks at Citeaux, Bernard, founded a daughter abbey at Clairvaux in 1116 and remained its abbot until his death in 1153. As a preacher, spiritual director and theologian, Bernard of Clairvaux was the leader of spiritual renewal in the twelfth century.

The Cistercians soon became the most influential religious order in the Church, surpassing Cluny, and eventually had six hundred monasteries founded from Citeaux. Not only were monasteries springing up, but also the parish clergy was being renewed by movements such as the Premonstratensians of Saint Norbert, a friend of Bernard.

Renewal was sweeping the Church, but the growing political influence and affluence of the Catholic Church, including the monasteries, led to the emergence of some groups who proclaimed to be living a truer and more radical gospel than the Church. The Cathars, medieval descendants of the Manichees, which had attracted Saint Augustine centuries earlier, emerged in southern France and were called Albigensians after the region of Albi located there. Other groups, such as the followers of Peter Valdes (the Waldensians) and the Humiliati in Italy, started out promoting reform and poverty in the Church but gradually drifted away from loyalty to the Catholic

Church and were condemned. Most of these groups were scandalized by the wealth or corruption they saw within the Catholic Church and wanted a more immediate, radical reform without full submission to the authority of the pope and the bishops.

Few groups, however, were as strict or radical as the new monastic orders—the Cistercians, Carthusians and the like. Reform was in the air, and these Catholic groups proved both the will for and the possibility of reform within the Church.

4. *Theology and Culture.*

The new life in the monasteries and cathedral schools brought new life to the Church in many ways. The solemn, round-arched Romanesque churches of earlier centuries gave way to the soaring spires of Gothic cathedrals. The earlier focus on Christ the King was replaced by images of the crucified and suffering Christ, perhaps reflecting the struggles of life and uncertainties of this period. People's piety was more personal and individualistic, and devotions to various saints and to Mary, Mother of God, flourished.

Worship was increasingly focused on the Eucharist, especially on the real presence of Christ in the Blessed Sacrament, which was confirmed by numerous Church councils. The term *transubstantiation* began to be used, describing the change of the host and the wine into, respectively, the Body and Blood of Christ in sacramental form. However, the focus in the medieval Church was more on gazing at the consecrated Host than on receiving the Lord in his Supper. The Mass took on more of the character of a drama to be observed, a passion play, rather than a communal meal.

The twelfth century also marked the beginning of Scholastic theology, the theology of the schools or universities. Reason was employed to understand the mysteries of faith and theology. Theologians wanted to form a synthesis using the teaching of the Bible, the early fathers of the Church and philosophy. Faith and reason, they believed, are not conflicting but complementary.

Leading the great theologians of this century was Saint Anselm of Canterbury (1033–1109), the Father of Scholasticism. Later came the brilliant but erratic Peter Abelard, whose errors were refuted by Saint Bernard of Clairvaux and Peter Lombard. Lombard's *Book of Sentences* was a systematic work that became the standard theology textbook for much of the thirteenth century. Mention should also be made of Gratian, a Camaldolese monk whose organization of the teachings and laws of the Catholic Church gave birth to the new science of canon law in the twelfth century.

In spite of the political struggles of the popes and the mixed results of the Crusades, God was clearly at work in the twelfth-century Church. The way was being prepared for the greatest century of spiritual, cultural and intellectual advancement in the history of Western civilization: the thirteenth century.

THE THIRTEENTH CENTURY

The thirteenth century was the flower of the Middle Ages and the height of Christendom. In almost every area of life, we see the influence of the Church and the advancement of culture and learning. Certainly there were dark moments, such as the Crusades and the Inquisition launched against heresies. But the light of the achievements of this century far outshines the darkness and illumines the Catholic Church even today.

1. *Popes and Councils.*

The thirteenth century gave rise to the most influential popes and some of the most successful councils of bishops in Christian history. The greatest pope was Innocent III (1198–1216), who managed to bring every secular ruler into submission to the Church by persuasion or by use of excommunication or interdict.

Yet worldly power was not Innocent's goal; he wanted full control of the Church so he could reform it. In 1215 he called the Fourth Lateran Council, which gathered more than four hundred bishops and eight hundred abbots and priors of religious houses, as well as representatives of the secular rulers. This council approved reform decrees that have affected the Church for centuries, such as the duty of Catholics to go to confession and receive Holy Communion at least once a year, normally during the Easter season. This council approved the term *transubstantiation* and also took measures, such as the Inquisition, to suppress heresies.

Innocent III, who was first to take the title Vicar of Christ, showed his great wisdom in his approach to the mendicant (poverty) movement. Many Christians were scandalized by the wealth that was flowing into the West as a result of the Crusades and the stabilization of society. These Christians wanted to live a simpler life of gospel poverty in imitation of Jesus Christ. Innocent recognized the necessity of this for the renewal of the Church and so approved the new orders of poor men (mendicants) founded by Francis of Assisi (1209) and Dominic Guzman (1215).

Innocent III also brought back to the Catholic Church other groups that had previously left, such as those known as the Poor Men of Lyons, led by Durand of Huesca, and the Poor Catholics. Some say Innocent III may have been more of a politician than a saint, but no one can deny that he did more than any other single pope of the period to strengthen and reform the Church.

In this compact history we cannot consider all the outstanding popes of this century, but there were two ecumenical councils that continued the reform of the Church: the First (1245) and Second (1274) Councils of Lyons. Both councils were held in France because of political pressures upon the pope in Rome. France was loyal to the pope, and saintly French kings, such as King Louis IX (1214–1270, canonized as Saint Louis), provided support and protection for the Church.

The last pope of the thirteenth century, Boniface VIII (1294–1303), is the ideal example of the achievement of the popes of that era. He continued to speak out against any interference of the state in Church affairs and proclaimed the ultimate authority of the pope over both the Church and the Christian social order in his famous bull *Unam Sanctam*. He called a tremendously successful Jubilee Year (or Holy Year) in 1300, the first of its kind, which drew over a million pilgrims to Rome. Papal authority reached its height in Innocent III and Boniface VIII.

2. *Crusades and Inquisition.*

The dark side of this century came with the efforts of the Church to hold on to Christian territory in the East and to stamp out heresy by force. The Fourth Crusade was called by

Innocent III in 1202, but without his permission it stopped in Constantinople to establish an emperor favorable to the West. The soldiers proceeded to plunder and ravage the beautiful city in 1204. "Even the Moslems," commented an observer, "would have been more merciful."[3] This created a tremendous bitterness in the hearts of Eastern Christians toward the Catholic Church, which is still not totally healed, and it discredited the whole crusading movement.

Innocent III was shocked by this but called for another Crusade at the Fourth Lateran Council to recover the city of Jerusalem. The Fifth Crusade (1218–1221) was moderately successful but failed to recapture Jerusalem. Frederick II managed to do this in the Sixth Crusade (1228–1229) by diplomacy, but this lasted only fifteen years. The Holy Land fell out of Western control when Muslim forces conquered the last Christian stronghold of Acre in 1291.

The lesson of these Crusades to capture the Holy Land has remained with the Church until the present day. Never again has the Catholic Church attempted to wage a war to capture territory, even the Holy Land, for the sake of Christ; nor has it condoned warfare among nations for this reason.

The Catholic Church was waging an even more important battle on another front in the thirteenth century. Because of wealth and corruption in the Church, certain groups, such as the Cathars and Waldensians, were drawing many people away from the Catholic Church in Europe and teaching them to deny the humanity of Christ, to reject the sacraments and to deny the spiritual authority of priests and of the Church. In response to this the Catholic Church established, in the thirteenth century, a legal procedure and tribunal to question those who were suspected of holding false, or heretical, teaching. This legal proceeding and tribunal was known as the Inquisition.

It is hard for many of us to understand this age in which hardly anyone believed in religious freedom or toleration. Persons living in a Catholic state or kingdom were expected to believe Catholic teaching. If they did not they were viewed as a threat to the society, and their souls as in danger of damnation. The Catholic Church viewed the Inquisition as a way of preserving the purity of the Catholic faith in a Catholic nation and of saving the souls of heretics from certain damnation by encouraging them to repent and accept the true faith. Even the limited use of torture by secular authorities came to be justified by the Church in the middle of the thirteenth century, on the principle that it was better for a person to suffer physical pain now for a brief time if it could save them from the eternal suffering of hell. (Note that the Roman law, preserved in the West by the Roman Emperor Justinian, sanctioned the use of torture to secure confessions.)

Contrary to popular belief, however, the goal of the Inquisition was to root out heresy by *converting* to the true faith those holding false beliefs. It is worthy of note that when Gregory IX established permanent inquisitors in 1233, he chose men from the new mendicant orders, especially the Dominicans, to lead people to conversion through the Inquisition.

3. *The Poverty Movement and the Mendicant Orders.*
One of the most widespread and influential movements of renewal in Christian history—stressing gospel simplicity and poverty—emerged amid the increasing wealth and political intrigue and turmoil of thirteenth-century Europe. Francis of

Assisi was born in 1181, son of a wealthy cloth merchant in this central Italian town. As Francis grew up, he was known for his love of parties and good times. Excited by the vision of the glory of knighthood, he went to war. After being taken prisoner, Francis was returned to Assisi, and his life began to change.

One day, praying in a small church at San Damiano, he heard Christ on the cross telling him to "rebuild my Church, which is falling into ruin." At first Francis thought he was to repair old churches, but the Lord showed him that he was to rebuild the Church simply by living a gospel life of utter poverty, in imitation of the poor Christ.

In 1209 Francis went with eleven companions to Rome to seek Innocent III's approval of their simple rule of life, which was nothing more than a few verses from the Gospels. Innocent was hesitant at first, but he then had a dream in which he saw Francis holding up the pillars of the Church of Rome. As a result Innocent approved Francis's rule and gave Francis and his followers permission to preach repentance wherever the local bishop gave them his permission. Saint Clare, a friend of Francis, founded the Poor Clares, a sister order to the Franciscans, which also flourished.

Francis's little band of followers grew to become the largest and most influential religious order of the Middle Ages, far surpassing the monastic orders in numbers and influence within a century. Even laypeople could follow this way of life as members of a "third order." The Franciscan witness was necessary in an age in which the Church was growing wealthy and some clergy remained corrupt. Francis did not look critically at the shortcomings of the Church or the clergy of this day, however, but remained totally loyal to the Church and loved it as God's work.

Despite his personal poverty and austerity, Francis of Assisi gloried in God's creation and had a special reverence for the humanity of Jesus. He invented the Christmas crèche, or manger scene. Francis also had a great love for the sacraments, especially the Eucharist, unlike many of the heretical groups of his day. Near his death God blessed Francis with the five wounds of Christ on his body, the stigmata—a fitting gift for one who so loved the crucified Christ. He was canonized a saint only two years after his death in 1226.

Dominic Guzman was a Spaniard born in 1170. After he was ordained a priest, he had a special concern for converting back to the Catholic Church those influenced by the Albigensian heresy (the Cathars). He realized that the people could be won back only by powerful preaching based on intellectual training combined with the witness of a poor and simple Christian life. His followers were recognized as the Order of Preachers by Pope Honorius III in 1216, after they adopted the rule of Saint Augustine.

Dominic loved God fervently. He often wept while preaching or celebrating Mass, and he called his followers to speak only *of* God or *with* God. He died in 1221 and was declared a saint in 1234.

Like the Franciscans, the Dominican Order became a great source of renewal, conversion of heretics and correction of intellectual error in the thirteenth century. Other religious orders, such as the newly formed Carmelites and the Augustinians, joined in spurring the Church on in this great century of renewal.

4. *New Learning, Theology and Culture.*

The thirteenth century also was the apex of the thought and culture of the Middle Ages. This began in the eleventh century with the founding of cathedral and urban schools. Around 1170 a new center of higher learning emerged—the university. The universities began as unions or guilds of scholars, which first attracted members of the clergy and were supported financially by the Church.

The first two great universities were founded at Paris (specializing in theology) and Bologna (law), but soon Oxford (1200), Cambridge (1209), Naples (1224), Salamanca (1220) and others followed. Medicine, law and theology were the fields of advanced study, and theology was called the queen of sciences. Theology had been studied mainly through critical reading *(lectio)* of sacred texts, but with the translation of the works of the Greek philosopher Aristotle from Arabic to Latin, a new, logical approach to theological study began. Theologians wanted to demonstrate how Christian faith was rational and that natural or worldly knowledge could fit into a Christian view of the world and of reality and would even support the Christian faith.

The three greatest theologians of the century came from the ranks of the new mendicant orders: a Franciscan, Bonaventure (1217–1274), and two Dominicans, Albert the Great (1200–1280) and Thomas Aquinas (1225–1274). Saint Bonaventure continued the long tradition of a mystical approach to theology, while employing reason subordinated to the authority of tradition and faith. Albert the Great was one of the first supporters of the thought of Aristotle, which had been initially banned by Rome from the universities because of its pagan origins. Albert's most renowned student, Thomas Aquinas, vigorously defended the value of Aristotle and constructed a system of thought that combined the Bible, the Church fathers and Aristotelian reasoning into a great, unified system of understanding Christian revelation as a whole through faith enlightened by reason. Aquinas's masterpiece was the *Summa Theologiae* (1266–1274), "The Summary of Theology," which is recognized as a pinnacle of genius and clarity. Contrary to popular belief, Thomas Aquinas never separated reason from faith. Reason enables mankind to understand more deeply the truths of faith revealed by God.

Thomas Aquinas was not the most popular theologian of his day though. John Duns Scotus (1266–1308), a Franciscan from Scotland, had a larger following. He disagreed with Saint Thomas on some important points but agreed with him on the intelligibility, or knowability, of all things.

The universities were not the only testimony to the advance of Western culture. Great writers, such as Dante Alighieri (1265–1321), emerged. Dante's *Divine Comedy*, an imaginative portrayal of hell, purgatory and heaven, is one of the greatest literary works of all time. Franciscan Roger Bacon (1214–1292) was a pioneer of experimental science. Gothic cathedrals soared to the heavens, and artists produced great works. The thirteenth century was truly the height of the Church's life and the height of Western culture in the Middle Ages.

the LATE MIDDLE AGES, REFORMATION *and* COUNTER-REFORMATION
(AD 1300–1650)

THE LATE MIDDLE AGES (1300–1500)

The thirteenth century was a time of fruition for Christianity and for the medieval Church and papacy. The period between 1300 and 1500 was, by comparison, a time of decline. This era of trouble was also marked by the fearsome Black Death, the bubonic plague that swept through Europe beginning in 1348 and wiped out one-third of its population. Yet God was at work in the Catholic Church and in society, in the midst of many challenges.

1. *The Avignon Papacy.*
The vibrant papacy of Boniface VIII (1294–1303) was followed by a period of more than seventy years, 1305–1376, in which the popes resided in Avignon, France. Clement V (pope from 1305 to 1314) moved to Avignon to escape the political pressures of

Italy, including the warring Roman families. King Philip of France promised peace and protection in return for a certain measure of influence on the policies of the pope. Although the Avignon popes did maintain a sense of their unique role as shepherds of *all* God's people, the rest of the world suspected that these popes had become the spokesmen of French interests. Indeed, the fact that eight popes during this period were French added fuel to their suspicions.

The Avignon papacy was criticized by noted Christian saints and poets, such as Petrarch, Saint Bridget of Sweden (1303–1373) and Saint Catherine of Siena (1347–1380). Both of these women saints were prophets whom God used powerfully to convince the pope to return to Rome. Bridget of Sweden was a wife and mother of eight children; her visions from God spurred the popes at Avignon to reform their luxurious lives and to care for the Church. Catherine of Siena pledged herself to virginity from her youth and became a Dominican of the Third Order. She devoted herself to service of the poor, until God began to give her messages (prophecies) about the Church. She convinced Pope Gregory XI to return from Avignon to Rome in 1376 and counseled his successor, Urban VI. Catherine was recently declared a doctor of the Church and is, with Saint Francis of Assisi, the patron of Italy.

2. *The "Great Schism" of the Popes (1378–1417).*
Pope Gregory XI died in 1378, soon after his return to Rome from Avignon. His death brought about an even greater crisis in the Church.

The cardinals gathered in Rome and, under some pressure from the Roman people, elected an Italian as Pope Urban VI.

To their surprise the mild-mannered Urban began to chastise the cardinals, constantly harping on them to reform their lives and even torturing some who opposed him. The French cardinals, claiming that the original election of Urban was invalid, fled Rome and elected a French "antipope," Clement VII. This began one of the saddest chapters in Catholic Church history, often called the "Great Schism." Two, and later three, men claimed to be the true pope, each supported by various nations and kingdoms.

The Church faced the pressing question of how to resolve this difficulty. None of the competing popes offered to resign, and the cardinals and bishops were divided in their loyalties. Some theologians, such as Frenchman Jean Gerson, chancellor of the University of Paris, had proposed earlier that the authority of an ecumenical council was greater than that of a pope, and he called for an ecumenical council of bishops to resolve the division. This was finally done. The Council of Constance (1414–1418) deposed two popes, persuaded the third to retire and elected a new pope, Martin V (1417), who was recognized by the whole Church. The Great Schism was ended but not before the prestige of the papacy had received a serious blow.

As a result of the Avignon papacy and the Great Schism, never again would we see in the Middle Ages popes who had the influence of Innocent III or Boniface VIII. Many Christians began to view the ecumenical council as having greater authority than the pope, though this was not true. The Council of Constance was an exception, not the rule, designed to respond to a state of emergency in the Church. The popes after this council continued to claim the same authority and role in the Church that popes had previously held.

3. *Challenges to the Church.*

The evident problems related to the papacy caused some Catholics to question and even deny the authority of the Church itself. A learned critic was John Wycliffe (1330–1384), an Oxford scholar who attacked the eucharistic doctrine of transubstantiation and other doctrines. Although he had done little serious study of Scripture, his translation of the Bible became one of his most well-known works. Wycliffe's ideas influenced a Czech reformer, John Hus (1369–1415). Hus was a Catholic priest (ordained 1400) who was excommunicated in 1412 for rejecting the Catholic understanding of the sacraments and denying the authority of the pope. Because of his attacks on the Church, the Council of Constance ordered him burned as a heretic in 1415.

Criticisms of the Church and rebellion against its authority increased in number and seriousness during this period. Even a branch of Franciscans who called themselves Spiritual Franciscans broke away from the Catholic Church because they could not accept the Church's authority to moderate the severity of Francis' rule concerning ownership of books or property. They predicted the imminent last age of the Church in their time.

Another challenge to the Church in the late Middle Ages was the decline of Scholastic theology, the theology of the schools or universities, which had reached its height in the days of Thomas Aquinas and John Duns Scotus. Although there continued to be some great and holy theologians in this period, such as the German Nicholas of Cusa (1401–1464), who wrote *The Vision of God*, Western theology began to decline. Theologians moved away from studying the Bible and the early Fathers of the Church and began to spend more time studying and commenting on each other's commentaries. Many of them engaged in dull speculation on unimportant issues—"How many angels can dance on the head of a pin?"— which heated the mind but chilled the heart. There was even a new approach to theology and philosophy called Nominalism, first championed by Englishman William of Ockham (1280–1349), that separated the realms of faith and reason instead of seeing them as complementary, as Thomas Aquinas and the other great Scholastics had done.

4. *Spiritual Awakening.*

As theology and philosophy became increasingly dry and detached from people's lives, one response was to look within man's heart to seek a spiritual awakening. The late Middle Ages was known for its Christian mystics, who sought to approach God through the heart more than through the intellect. Meister Eckehart (1260–1327), a German Dominican, was one of the first and most influential mystics, although some of his doctrine was suspected by Church authorities. Eckehart was accused of heresy in 1326, a year before his death.

John Tauler (1300–1361) and Henry Suso (1295–1366) were both Dominican priests and followers of Eckehart. Tauler taught that our lives must reflect the life of the Blessed Trinity. Suso's *Little Book of Eternal Wisdom* was called the finest fruit of German mysticism.

Mystical writer John van Ruysbroeck (1293–1381) is considered by some to be the greatest Flemish saint. England could boast of many mystics: Julian of Norwich (1342–1416) wrote her *Revelations of Divine Love*; Walter Hilton's (d. 1395) *Scale of*

Perfection was the most clear and balanced statement of the interior life in the late Middle Ages; an unknown author wrote *Cloud of Unknowing* in the late fourteenth century.

Another response to the abstract dryness of the theology of the time was a movement called the *Devotio Moderna*, the modern devotion, which emerged in the late fourteenth century and spread through the fifteenth century. This devotional writing avoided all theological disputes but was not mystical. It was a practical method that reflected on the life of Jesus in a systematic way. Thomas à Kempis's *Imitation of Christ* is the classic work from this school.

Gerard Groote (1340–1384) was one of the *Devotio Moderna's* great advocates, and he inspired the founding of a lay congregation called the Brethren of the Common Life and a religious order, the Canons of Saint Augustine of Windesheim. Some other religious orders were reformed in this period, such as the Franciscan Observatines, led by Saint Bernardine of Siena (d. 1444) and Saint John of Capistrano (d. 1456). Certain orders of Benedictine monks and Augustinian canons were reformed too, including the one Martin Luther later joined.

Among Eastern Christians the method of prayer called *hesychasm*, or prayer of the heart, became popular in the thirteenth and fourteenth centuries. Gregory Palamas (1296–1359), a great mystical theologian of the Eastern Church, and others advocated this form of prayer, which consisted of a constant, internal repetition of the name of Jesus (or of a short phrase like "Lord Jesus Christ, Son of God, have mercy on me"). Such prayers became rhythmically connected with one's breathing. The goal was to be praying constantly, always focused on God.

A collection of writings of the Eastern Fathers of the Church known as the *Philokalia* provided the basis for this spirituality.

Also included among the mystics and visionaries of the late Middle Ages is Saint Joan of Arc (1412–1431). Beginning at age thirteen, Joan claimed to hear the voices of angels and saints, who revealed to her a mission to help the king of France, Charles VII, wrest France from British control. Having determined that her visions were authentic, the king allowed her to lead an army into Orleans. The army was victorious, but the king handed Joan over to the English, who unjustly accused her of heresy and burned her at the stake. Twenty-five years after her death, Joan was cleared of all charges by the Church, and in 1920 she was declared a saint. Joan of Arc was a truly unusual and remarkable saint for troubled times. God spoke messages and revealed himself to the faithful in many surprising ways.

5. *Background Causes of the Protestant Reformation.*
There were sparks of spiritual awakening in the late Middle Ages, but the tragedy that led to the Reformation was that spiritual reform and renewal were not firmly rooted in the mainstream of the Catholic Church. There were obstacles to the renewal God desired, from the popes to common people. The popes were faced with the rise of nationalism and with princes who would only allow the reform of the Church in their territories for a price. The popes were forced to negotiate concordats, or treaties, with the nations, and these governments made vast revenues from manipulating the Church.

As the financial situation of the popes grew worse, they developed ways to increase papal revenues that had many bad effects. In this age many secular rulers also became bishops or abbots in order to control the Church and receive its revenues. The popes tried to get money back from the secular rulers by setting a high papal tax on these ecclesiastical offices. If the princes wanted to control the Church, they would at least have to pay for it. This practice of simony—the selling of spiritual goods and Church offices—was widely condemned as immoral. Some secular rulers purchased the right to hold two or more Church offices (pluralism) and then never cared for the people but hired others to do it (absenteeism).

So the bishops of the Church were often the wealthy or the nobility who had little care for the Church of God's people but used their office to their own advantage. When they needed to raise money, they would collect it from fees at pilgrimage sites or through the selling of indulgences. Indulgences were granted by the Church as a pledge of freedom from the effects of sin (that is, punishment in purgatory) after a person died. Indulgences were supposed to be granted in recognition of a person's prayer or good works, but toward the end of the Middle Ages, they were peddled like merchandise. The Dominican indulgence-seller Tetzel, who sparked Luther's protest against the Church, was reported to have chanted, "As soon as a coin in the coffer rings, the soul from purgatory springs."[1]

The lower clergy (priests) and deacons of the Catholic Church also suffered from lack of education and widespread corruption. Many were poor and worldly, and they lived with women in violation of the Church's law of celibacy. Even the mendicant orders had largely lost their fervor and were the brunt of the satire of the humanists for rivaling thieves and legitimate beggars in their constant quest for money.

Ordinary Catholics too were generally untouched by the streams of renewal in the Church. Their Christian life often focused on external devotions to saints or Mary, going on pilgrimages and gaining indulgences, without an understanding of the more basic truths of the Catholic faith. With sound teaching from priests and bishops either rare or nonexistent, the common Catholic could hardly be blamed for lack of understanding.

How would the Catholic Church be reformed in such a sad situation? The popes were preoccupied with political affairs, and most of them from the middle of the fifteenth century onward were also concerned with supporting the Renaissance, the new wave of learning and culture that was sweeping through Europe. In some ways this was a very good thing. The Renaissance popes wanted to show that the Church supported learning, art, music and literature. Pope Julius II laid the foundation of St. Peter's Church in Rome and hired Bernini, Raphael and Michelangelo—some of the greatest artists in the world at the time—to provide altars, statues and paintings for it. Again, this cost money and diverted the popes' attention away from the desperate spiritual condition of the Church.

Some churchmen and princes urged the popes to call an ecumenical council to reform the Church. After much hesitation, fearing that a council would usurp the pope's authority or be controlled by a secular ruler, Pope Julius II finally called the Fifth Lateran Council in Rome in 1512. It concluded in 1517, under Pope Leo X, on the eve of the Protestant Reformation. The council passed many needed reform decrees that might have prevented the Protestant Reformation, but because of the shortsightedness and worldliness of Pope Leo X (pope from

1513 to 1521), most of the council's reform decrees were never put into effect. Also, some of the Church's bishops had little interest in reform.

One might wonder whether any Catholics were speaking out in favor of reform. Certainly some were. Besides the men and women leading the spiritual awakening and reforming religious orders, there was also a group of Christians known as the Humanists. Led by the scholarly Erasmus of Rotterdam (1465–1536), the Humanists were learned Catholics who were saddened by the decline in Scholastic theology and the rise of Nominalism. They decided to refound Catholic thought on the Bible and writings of the early Fathers of the Church. Erasmus wrote extensively in these areas, as well as writing humorous satires poking fun at the distortions of Catholic life.

Humor and satire were not enough to reform the Church, however, nor was Erasmus's brilliance as a classical scholar. The condition of the Church had reached the point that made it possible for the fiery temperament of Martin Luther to ignite a reformation destined to shake and divide Western Christianity.

THE PROTESTANT REFORMATION (1517–1650)

1. *Martin Luther (1480–1546).*

One historian has written, "The Reformation came not so much because Europe was irreligious as because it was religious."[2] Martin Luther was a gruff German of peasant stock who sparked the religious idealism of the people of Europe. He was also an Augustinian monk of a strict order and had studied hard to become a professor of Scripture at the University of

Wittenberg in Germany. As a monk he had found no peace in trying to clear his guilty conscience through penance and self-denial but experienced freedom when he realized that man is justified by faith alone, as Paul explains in his Letter to the Romans. This was the key that led Luther to post his Ninety-Five Theses on Indulgences on the chapel door at Wittenberg in 1517. He renounced the Catholic dependence on good works of any sort, including indulgences, to gain salvation or the remission of sin.

The irony of the Protestant Reformation is that much of what Luther believed and taught was authentic Catholic doctrine that had been distorted by abuses and incorrect practices in the Church, such as the mercenary selling of indulgences. Unfortunately, Luther's criticism of real abuses was not heeded. Pope Leo X simply instructed Luther's superiors in his order to correct him as a rebellious monk who was questioning the Church's legitimate authority to grant indulgences.

At first Luther had no intention of leaving the Catholic Church, but he also refused to retract his statements until he was given a hearing. In 1519 he went to Leipzig to meet with theologian Johannes Eck. Eck led Luther to deny the authority of the popes and of ecumenical councils and to stand on the Bible alone as his sole authority. (One of Luther's great achievements later was to translate the Bible into German, so that, with the invention of the printing press, German Lutherans could have access to the Bible in their own language.)

At this point Luther realized that he could no longer remain a Catholic; so he wrote three treatises denouncing the authority of the Catholic Church and the popes, rejecting the sacraments of the Church (except baptism, the Lord's

Supper—Eucharist—and penance) and calling for the Christian princes of Germany to rise up and start their own national church. This is exactly what happened. Most of the German princes were eager to escape the authority and taxation of Rome, so they supported Luther and nominated their own bishops of the new Lutheran Church.

The Catholic Church, with the bull *Exsurge Domine* (1520), formally warned Martin Luther of serious doctrinal errors. After Luther responded by burning the bull and some of his Catholic books, he was excommunicated in January 1521. The young emperor Charles V called Luther to the Diet of Worms in 1521, where Luther still refused to recant. His rejection of the authority of the Catholic Church is a great tragedy, not only because it began another division of the body of Christ but also because of the positive and necessary work of reform that he may have been able to accomplish within the Catholic Church had he remained part of it.

Because this book is primarily instruction in the history of the Catholic Church, we will not go further in describing the development of the Lutheran Church. However, it is enough to say that Lutheranism was the most Catholic form of Protestantism, because Luther retained many aspects of Catholic belief and tradition, *except* those things that he felt were directly contradicted by the Bible. The other streams of the Reformation (with the exception of Anglicanism) were to depart even more radically from Catholicism.

2. *Jean Calvin (1509–1564)*.

Jean Calvin was of French origin, and after studying theology and law in Paris as a young man, he was suddenly converted to the principles of the Reformation begun by Luther. Eventually

Calvin settled in Geneva, Switzerland, where he combined the authority of the city and the Church, with primacy given to the Church. In this theocracy Calvin forged a model of strict and austere Christian life comparable to the discipline of the medieval monasteries. John Knox (1513–1572) of Scotland, after visiting Geneva, called it "the most perfect school of Christ that ever was on the earth since the days of the apostles"[3] and proceeded to bring Calvinism back to Scotland as the Presbyterian Church.

Calvin's great written work is his *Institutes of the Christian Religion*, the basis of the theology of the Reformed tradition. Calvin rejected all beliefs not explicitly found in the Bible and focused his followers' faith on the Word of God alone. His church buildings were plain and white, without altars, statues, images, organ music or stained-glass windows. All vestiges of Catholicism except the Bible and a table for the Lord's Supper were stripped away. Calvin's most widely debated doctrine is predestination, claiming that God has predetermined from the beginning who will be saved and who will be damned, apparently leaving no place for human effort, merit or will in attaining salvation. The elect will inevitably manifest the fruit of their election through their upright and productive Christian lives.

Calvin's great hope of converting his native France was partially fulfilled with the rise of the Huguenots (French Calvinists) in the seventeenth century.

3. *The "Radical Reformation."*

Jean Calvin had departed more radically from the Catholic faith than Martin Luther. However, there were some groups of the Protestant Reformation that departed even further from their Catholic heritage. Huldreich Zwingli (1484–1531) started a church in the city of Zurich, Switzerland, that taught that the Lord's Supper was simply a commemorative meal and that there is no real reception of Christ in the Eucharist. Luther bitterly disagreed with Zwingli on this point at the Colloquy at Marburg in 1529.

Before his death in battle in 1531, Zwingli ordered the drowning of a group of men in Zurich who insisted on rebaptizing adults and who taught that only an adult baptism, or a believer's baptism, is valid. These Anabaptists (rebaptizers) had gone too far for Zwingli. They fled from Zurich to establish small, tightly knit communities in isolated regions of Moravia to the east.

Anabaptist was a name given to a wide variety of groups in this period who held what Catholics and Protestants alike thought were very radical beliefs. One Anabaptist, Thomas Münzer, led a wild revolt of peasants, and the "King of Munster," John of Leiden, took over a city and allowed unrestrained sexual activity there. These few irresponsible Anabaptists led to the merciless persecution of some very serious Christians, such as the Hutterites of Moravia, who shared all their goods in common and led peaceful, industrious lives, and the Mennonites of Holland, who were pacifists and extremely austere. There were probably more Anabaptists who died for their faith in this period than any other Christian group. They were persecuted by both Catholics and Protestants, and they refused to defend themselves by force.

4. *The Reformation in England.*

You may have noted that the previous three streams of the Protestant Reformation—Lutheranism, Calvinism and the Anabaptists—are progressively less similar to the Catholic Church from which they broke away. Once the Catholic principle of *unity of faith* was replaced by the Protestant principle of *purity of faith*, more and more splinter groups or churches formed, each claiming to be more pure and faithful to the gospel of Jesus Christ than other groups. Based on this principle, the Reformation inevitably split the Church into many segments and divided bodies. However, this observation would not disturb many Protestants who view the church that Jesus founded as an *invisible, spiritual* reality comprised of all who believe in Christ rightly in their hearts and not as a *visible, historical* reality existing in unified form in the world, as Catholics understand the Church. This is one important aspect of the difference in understanding of the Church between most Protestants and Catholics.

The church of the Reformation that was most Catholic in its outlook, at least at first, was the Church of England, the Anglican Church. This church was established by King Henry VIII of England, seemingly a devout Catholic, who had been named a "Defender of the Faith" by a previous pope. Henry requested an annulment of his marriage to Catherine of Aragon, because she bore him no male heir. Pope Clement VII refused to grant Henry the annulment, as Henry had received a papal dispensation to marry Catherine in the first place, for she had been married to Henry's brother.

After Cardinal Wolsey, archbishop of Canterbury, failed to influence the pope to grant the king's request, Henry dismissed Wolsey in 1529 and appointed a trusted friend, the Catholic lawyer Sir Thomas More, to the position of chancellor of England. Thomas More, as a Catholic loyal to the pope, made it clear that he could only accept the position if he was not to be involved with the question of King Henry's marriage. When

Henry proclaimed himself supreme head of the Church of England in 1534 and severed ties with Rome, More refused to swear the oath of allegiance to the king under this title and also refused to explain why.

Legally More's life should have been safe, since English law proclaims silence to indicate assent. However, Henry refused to let this legal "loophole" allow the opposition of such a popular and respected statesman as Thomas More, and so More was beheaded in 1535, as a martyr upholding the Catholic faith. John Fisher, bishop of Rochester, was also beheaded, and both were later declared saints by the Catholic Church.

Even though the Church of England began by diverging from Roman Catholicism on only one point—the governing authority of the pope—it increasingly became subject to Calvinistic influences under later rulers and became more Protestant in belief. Catholics in the sixteenth and seventeenth centuries came to be bitterly persecuted in England. Papists were viewed as political subversives trying to undermine the state, especially after an ill-fated attempt by a Catholic, Guy Fawkes, to blow up the British Parliament in 1604 (the Gunpowder Plot). Over the centuries, though, a large portion of the Church of England swung back to a more Catholic brand of Christianity, and thus many Anglicans today (particularly High Church Anglicans) view themselves not as Protestants but as true Catholics.

THE COUNTER-REFORMATION (1500–1650)

There is no question that the Catholic Church was in dire need of reform in 1500, on the eve of the Protestant Reformation.

There were many Catholics who had been striving to reform their Church before Luther and had even achieved some success. Cardinal Ximenez de Cisneros, Catholic leader of Spain from 1495 to 1517, brought about many reforms in the Catholic Church in Spain. In Italy the Oratory of Divine Love, established in Genoa in 1497, was a society founded by laypeople to seek holiness and to serve others. Catholic Humanists Erasmus of Rotterdam and John Colet of England openly lamented the spiritual confusion and decay in the Catholic Church. The Fifth Lateran Council passed many reform decrees.

Most Catholics, though, including the popes, did not take the reform of their Church seriously until the Protestant reformers spoke out boldly and left the unity of the Catholic Church. One positive result of the Protestant Reformation is that it began a more diligent effort of reform and renewal within the Catholic Church. Even though Catholics cannot agree that there is ever any justification for dividing the one Church of Jesus (and so Catholics vigorously opposed the Protestant reformers), the Catholic leaders and people of the sixteenth century came to realize their own need to repent for failing to reform. They began the work of renewal within the Catholic Church in earnest.

1. *Reform Through Religious Orders.*

The Catholic Reformation was ignited by the founding of new religious orders and groups, as well as the renewal of existing orders. One of the central concerns of the Catholic Reformation was the quest for a holy, zealous and celibate clergy to lead the Church in its reform. The religious order that led the way was the Society of Jesus, or the Jesuits, founded by Saint Ignatius of Loyola in 1534 and recognized by the pope in 1540.

Ignatius was a Spanish soldier whose right leg was shattered in battle in 1521. While recovering, Ignatius read the life of Christ and a book of the saints, and these gave him such spiritual joy that he decided to spend his life serving God in the Catholic Church. After obtaining a good education, which later became a great apostolate of his order, Ignatius chose six men to join in a brotherhood—including Francis Xavier, the great missionary. Despite being constantly suspected by the Inquisition, Ignatius's order was finally approved by the pope.

Obedience to the Catholic Church and to the pope in particular was a special mark of the Jesuits. The order began by educating the illiterate and poor, but within a few years it was educating princes and kings as well. The Jesuits also became great missionaries; Francis Xavier brought the gospel of Jesus Christ to India and Japan beginning in 1541. Later the battle to defend the Catholic faith became a primary work of the Jesuits. Saint Peter Canisius of Germany wrote a catechism of the Catholic faith that was praised even by Protestants for its biblical basis and clarity. Saint Robert Bellarmine was a great theologian and a leader at the reform Council of Trent. Finally, Saint Ignatius's *Spiritual Exercises* (1541) became a classic of Christian spirituality and the basis of the Jesuits' great work in retreats and spiritual discernment.

Although the Society of Jesus became the largest and most influential religious order of the Catholic Reformation, many other orders were founded that made important contributions to renewing the Catholic Church. Among these were the Capuchins—a reformed branch of the Franciscans that became second only to the Jesuits in reforming influence—the Theatines, Somaschi and Barnabites. Orders of religious women, such as the Ursuline Sisters (1535), also had a powerful effect in renewing the Catholic Church, as did the oratories—associations founded for prayer, study and service that included laypeople. Saint Philip Neri's oratory, founded in Rome in 1575, was very well known and effective. Philip Neri, the cheerful saint, is a patron saint of youth and an inspiration to all Christians. For his work in renewing the Church in the Eternal City, he is called "the second apostle of Rome."

2. *The Reform Council:*
The Council of Trent (1545–1563) and Its Effects.

In spite of the positive influence of these groups, the Catholic Church still needed to come together to seek reform by means of an ecumenical council, a gathering of all the Catholic bishops. The bishops needed to decide together how to respond to the Protestant Reformation and what steps were necessary to reform and renew the Catholic Church. After many delays Pope Paul III opened the Council of Trent in 1545.

Even though many Catholic leaders, such as Cardinal Gaspar Contrarini, had sought to reconcile the Catholic Church and various Protestant groups, by 1545 differences between Catholics and Protestants had grown too deep and hurtful to hope for a reunification of Christ's Church in the West. So the Council of Trent began by clarifying and defining exactly what the Catholic Church taught, especially points challenged by Protestantism. Trent affirmed the Catholic belief in seven sacraments instituted by Christ; man's justification by faith shown by the fruits of faith *and* good works or charity; the revelation of God to his Church through both the Bible *and* apostolic tradition; and the nature of the Mass as a perpetuation or re-presentation of Jesus' *one* sacrifice on Calvary.

The Council of Trent also corrected many of the abuses criticized by Catholics and Protestants alike. The office of indulgence-seller was abolished, and proper devotion to Mary and the saints was promoted. One of the most important achievements of the Council of Trent was the establishment of the seminary system. Each diocese was to establish a seminary for the formation and education of priests. This resulted in a more educated and pure-hearted Catholic diocesan clergy who could preach the gospel and be examples of Christ to their people.

There had been many other ecumenical councils concerned with the reform of the Catholic Church before the Council of Trent. Trent was different because most of its reforms were actually carried out and put into effect. Even though many rulers and nations had left the Catholic Church as a result of the Protestant Reformation, the ones who remained Catholic generally were supportive of the renewal of Catholicism. Most of the popes elected in the later sixteenth century and onward had the reform and spiritual renewal of the Catholic Church as their first priority, as did many bishops, such as Saint Charles Borromeo, archbishop of Milan from 1565 to 1585. The Spirit of Christ and his Good News flowed more freely through the Catholic Church and was evident in both the earthly head of the Church and its members.

Sadly, one result of the Protestant Reformation was that the Catholic Church seemed to become less catholic or universal. It had to tighten its discipline and redefine itself, withdrawing from the world to a degree in order to determine its own lifestyle and identity. Some people say that the Catholic Church became a fortress church—more certain of its identity but more defensive because of the opposition of Protestantism.

Another way to look at the Catholic Church after the Reformation, though, is to see it as a church that was purified and renewed and that reflected more clearly the life of Christ. There was a flowering, a new springtime, of faith and devotion among many Catholics. Devotion to Mary and the saints was purified and renewed. The Council of Trent encouraged Catholics to receive Holy Communion frequently—at least once a week—and to receive forgiveness of their sins in the sacrament of penance often. Adoration of the Lord in the Blessed Sacrament was encouraged through benediction and forty hours services. Even though Mass continued to be said in Latin rather than in the language of the people, missals and other devotional aids helped people to pray when they attended Mass.

3. Catholic Mystics and Activist Saints.

This great age of renewal in the Catholic Church also was marked by an abundance of great mystics and activist saints.

Mysticism is the direct apprehension of God by the mind or soul, knowing God in the heart. Catholic leaders were cautious about mysticism, fearing too much emphasis on one's own experience or feelings and possible delusion by the devil or evil spirits. Nonetheless, God raised up many great Catholic mystics in this period, especially in Spain.

Saint Teresa of Avila (1515–1582) was a Spaniard who joined the Carmelite order at the age of twenty and led a rather ordinary religious life until 1556. At that time, after about fifteen years of dryness in prayer, Teresa had what was called a second conversion and began to experience mystical prayer—sometimes accompanied by visions and voices. She became a vigorous reformer of the Carmelite Order, founding the discalced (barefoot) Carmelites and seventeen vibrant religious houses before her death. Her books, including her autobiography, *The Way of Perfection* and *The Interior Castle*, are regarded as spiritual classics.

Saint Teresa greatly influenced another Spanish Carmelite, John de Yepes (1542–1591), now known as Saint John of the Cross. A great mystic, John suffered much during his lifetime and describes an approach to God through darkness and suffering in his works *Dark Night of the Soul, Ascent of Mount Carmel, Spiritual Canticle* and *Living Flame of Love*.

The French Catholic Church after the Reformation produced such well-known saints as Saint Francis de Sales (1567–1622), Saint Jeanne de Chantal (1572–1641) and Saint Vincent de Paul (1581–1660). Saint Francis de Sales, bishop of Geneva, Switzerland, from 1602 to 1622, was noted as a great pastor and a man of intellect and wisdom. His books, *An Introduction to the Devout Life* and *Treatise on the Love of God*, are spiritual guides for average people who want to become saints through the means of everyday life. Through his writing and preaching, Francis attracted thousands of Swiss Protestants back to the Catholic faith. He was proclaimed doctor of the Church and has three religious orders under his patronage.

One of Francis de Sales's close friends was Jeanne de Chantal, a widow who, with Francis, founded the Order of the Visitation in 1610. This order of sisters first worked with the poor and sick and then devoted themselves to prayer. By the time of her death, Saint Jeanne de Chantal had founded eight houses of sisters.

Saint Vincent de Paul had a tremendous zeal for reform and a great love of the poor. His Congregation of the Mission was a religious order that promoted the holiness of the French clergy. He also helped found the Sisters of Charity in 1633, the first Catholic order of sisters who lived a fully active life in the world, ministering among the poor and sick. Vincent was so active in charitable works of all sorts, such as ransoming slaves from galley ships, that he is the Catholic patron of all works of charity.

4. *Catholic Missionary Outreach.*

Besides this wealth of mystics, preachers and activist saints, the Catholic Reformation marks the beginning of a great period of missionary expansion of the Catholic Church to all nations. There had been a few missionary outreaches in the Middle Ages, such as Franciscan John of Montecorvino's planting the Catholic Church in Beijing, China, in 1307. However, Christianity was basically restricted to Europe until Christopher Columbus's discovery of the New World in 1492 and the Portuguese explorations of India. Then the missionary fervor of the Catholic Church exploded.

Saint Francis Xavier, S.J., first brought the Christian message to the Far East in 1542, and he was soon followed by Jesuits Matteo Ricci, who led an expedition to China in 1581, and Robert de Nobili, who adopted the lifestyle of a Brahmin to bring the Catholic faith to India. The most successful Catholic missionary effort in Asia was in the Philippines, where a bishop was established in 1581. Today Catholics comprise 80 percent of the Philippine population.

To encourage this missionary effort, Pope Gregory XV formed the Sacred Congregation of the Propagation of the Faith in 1622. Whenever explorers were sent out from Catholic countries, so were Catholic missionaries. Despite the cruelty of some of the Spanish conquerors of the Western Hemisphere, the missionaries often fought for the rights of the native peoples of Central and South America. They worked in teaching and caring for the native peoples of the New World, as well as converting them.

Shining lights of the Spanish Catholic mission were Dominican Bartholomew Las Casas (1474–1566), who crossed the Atlantic fourteen times to secure legal rights for the native peoples from the Spanish government, and Saint Turibio, archbishop of Lima, Peru, from 1580 to 1606, who pushed through laws to defend the liberties of natives and blacks, educated them and translated textbooks into their language.

In 1588 Jesuit Joseph Acosta wrote the first modern theory of world evangelism and encouraged a priesthood from among the native peoples. The Jesuits also established villages, known as the Reductions, among the people of Paraguay, which were very successful centers of Christian communal life and worship.

In North America the French colonized Canada, and the Jesuits and Franciscans were active in evangelizing the Huron, Algonquin and Iroquois tribes. The blood of martyrs marks the efforts to bring some of these peoples to Christ, such as the heroic and bloody deaths of Jesuits Isaac Jogues (martyred by the Iroquois in 1646), John de Brebeuf and others. John de Brebeuf preached to more than ten thousand Huron Indians over the years 1625 to 1640 and helped convert the majority of the Huron nation. The Spanish explorers went to what is now the western United States, where Jesuit missionary Father Eusebio Kino worked in New Mexico and Franciscan priest Junípero Serra founded missions along the coast of California, many of which still exist today.

SUMMARY

What was the net effect of the Catholic and Protestant Reformations? The Catholic Church had begun to reform through the grace of God. Catholic reform emphasized "three *Ds*": devotion (new fervor in worship), discipline (reform of abuses and purified Catholic life) and doctrine (clarification of Catholic beliefs). Historian Thomas Bokenkotter comments on the results of this reform:

> By the end of the Council of Trent in 1563, Protestantism had already established its sway over half of Europe. This trend was reversed, however, during the remainder of the century. With the publication of Trent's decrees and the upsurge of new vitality in the Catholic Church—manifested especially in the Jesuits and the regenerated papacy—the Catholic Church began to recover large blocs of territory. Poland turned back to Catholicism; large parts of Germany, France, and the southern Netherlands were likewise restored to communion with the Holy See, while Protestantism made no significant gains after 1563. And overseas Catholic mission gains compensated for the losses suffered in Europe.[4]

While the gospel was being spread to the ends of the earth by Catholic missionaries in the first half of the seventeenth century, Europe was engaged in bitter wars of religion between Catholics and Protestants and among Protestant nations. The last of these religious wars took place in Germany. The Thirty Years' War (1618–1648) was brought to an end by the Treaty of Westphalia (1648), which granted Catholics, Lutherans and Calvinists equality before the law in Germany.

In reality, each nation or region within a nation had its own particular Christian "church," and those people of another Christian faith within that territory often were persecuted either directly or indirectly. Even though there were truces from direct conflict, Christian Europe was divided into warring camps in which religion was a key factor. This sad situation helped give rise to a search for a "reasonable religion" in the next period of Christianity.

Nonetheless, within each segment of the divided Church, there were many places where the Good News of Jesus Christ burned brightly. The Catholic Church, certainly, looked forward with hope to the strengthening of Catholic life in Europe and to the further spread of the Catholic faith in Christ throughout the world. The Catholic Church had met its greatest challenge to date and had survived with renewed vigor.

the CATHOLIC CHURCH CONFRONTS *the* MODERN WORLD
(AD 1650–1900)

THE MODERN WORLD

The period from the middle of the seventeenth century to the present time is a new era in human history, often called the modern world. What is different about this time?

The life of Western civilization changed because of the emergence of modern science, of a new approach to philosophy based solely on reason and of the rearrangement of the whole political system in most of Europe that eventually affected much of the world. The foundation of Western society was shaken to its base. The Catholic Church and all Christians were subjected to another severe test, which in many respects is still going on today.

1. *The Emergence of Science and Technology.*

The seventeenth and eighteenth centuries are often called the Age of Enlightenment. One aspect of the Enlightenment was a new view of the order of the universe. Nicholas Copernicus (1473–1543) proposed that the sun is the center of the planetary system and the earth revolves around it. Although this overturned the traditional view of the Greek astronomer Ptolemy, Galileo Galilei (1564–1642) demonstrated through observation that Copernicus was correct. The modern science of astronomy was born.

Not long afterward others, such as Englishmen Sir Isaac Newton and Robert Boyle, were pioneering the new sciences of physics and chemistry. These sciences not only revolutionized the understanding of the physical universe but also gave birth to the application of science to practical problems—technology—which led to an industrial revolution in England and eventually in all European nations. Progress based on science and technology became a major goal of Western society.

2. *The New Philosophy.*

Another aspect of the Enlightenment was a new approach to philosophy based solely on human reason. Frenchman René Descartes (1596–1650) taught that every concept should be questioned or doubted until reason could prove its validity. This philosophy, emphasizing the ability of human reason to determine the truth of all things, is called *rationalism.* Later philosophers challenged this exaltation of reason and proposed philosophies based on, or including, human experience or the observable natural order of things.

One thing that most of these philosophies had in common was that faith of any sort, including Christian faith, was rejected as a component of philosophy. For many of these philosophers, persons who based their lives or beliefs primarily on faith were unenlightened and living in a past age of human development.

3. *New Experiments in the Political Order.*

The modern world also experienced great political upheavals as new experiments in various forms of government were consciously undertaken by rulers or compelled by the people. The idea of a king who governed by divine right or authority was rejected. The Christian churches played less and less of an active role in directing and shaping the political life of European nations. In fact, the Catholic Church and other Christian churches often became either victims of political manipulation by secular rulers or institutions viewed as outmoded and given no place in the political order; some were even suppressed.

4. *Secularization.*

Overall the modern age is one in which Christianity has been allowed increasingly less room for public expression and influence in the political, cultural and intellectual life of the West. The Christian religion has not been abandoned but relegated to the private sphere of one's personal life. This process of the privatization of religion and the exclusion of religion from the public life of society (including politics, philosophy, science, literature, the arts, the public media and other aspects) is called *secularization.* This process is still going on, but it finds its roots in the so-called Enlightenment of the seventeenth and eighteenth centuries. As we proceed now to present the story of the Catholic Church in this period, we will consider the Catholic response to this Enlightenment and to the modern world.

FROM 1650 TO
THE FRENCH REVOLUTION (1789)

1. *The Appeal to Reason.*

In some ways the condition of Christianity in the sixteenth and seventeenth centuries ushered in the Enlightenment. The people of Europe were tired of wars of religion, and some philosophers argued that the only basis for restoring unity and peace to Europe was to find a common basis of agreement, either in a "reasonable religion" purged of all divisive dogmas or in reason itself. Immanuel Kant (1724–1804) wrote, "'Have courage to use your own reason'—that is the motto of enlightenment."[1]

Some philosophers, such as the German Gottfried Leibniz (1646–1716), were optimistic about the prospect of discovering and agreeing upon a "rational religion" that would again unify Europe. The Englishman Lord Herbert of Cherbury presented five propositions that would be the substance of the new religion of reason, popularly known as Deism. According to the Deists, God established the laws of the universe and set it in motion—like a clockmaker winding up his clock—but after that he does not intervene directly in the affairs of his creation. Obviously, this directly contradicts Christian belief in divine revelation, miracles worked by God and the incarnation of God in Jesus Christ. Yet some Deists claimed that they were still Christians.

Some philosophers launched a direct attack against the Catholic Church and Christianity, notably the French satirist and philosopher Voltaire (1694–1778). Voltaire, more than any other person, made it fashionable to be a mocker of Christianity and a cynic regarding the Catholic Church particularly. As a result of Voltaire's approach, gentlemen's societies of free thinkers, called Freemasons, arose in France and even attracted some priests.

A less obvious attack on Christianity was the new scientific study of the Bible, which sought to analyze and evaluate the Bible with the same literary and historical methods as would be applied to any other book. In itself there was nothing wrong with this approach, except that skeptics, like French philosopher Pierre Bayle and others, concluded from it that the Bible was no different from any other book.

How did the Catholic Church respond to these intellectual challenges? Blaise Pascal (1623–1662), the great French mathematician, argued against Descartes by insisting on God's approach to man through revelation, religious experience and the Judeo-Christian tradition as well as through reason. He believed in "the God of Abraham, Isaac and Jacob,…the God of Jesus Christ," not in the abstract god of the philosophers.

In England there were many churchmen of the Anglican communion who defended the truth of Christianity, such as Bishop Joseph Butler. Unfortunately, there were no Catholics in France or elsewhere who had the same ability to refute Voltaire, Diderot and later philosophers who were undermining Christianity. The popes vehemently rejected the position that the Bible could be interpreted in exactly the same way as any other literary writing, because it is God's Word to his Church and not merely a human word.

2. The Catholic Church and Science.

The Catholic understanding of the book of Genesis at this time appeared to be in conflict with the astronomical findings of Copernicus and Galileo. The Roman Inquisition condemned their findings in 1616 and 1623, respectively, as attacks on the inerrancy of Scripture. The Catholic Church had not yet drawn the distinction that we do today between scientific and historical propositions in the Bible and the biblical teachings regarding religious truth.

Today Catholics recognize that the Bible was not intended by its authors to explain scientific phenomena nor to depict actual events from a merely historical perspective. However, the biblical teaching regarding religious truth—about mankind's relationship with God and neighbor—is always infallibly true and inerrant. The Church's earlier confusion about this is understandable, since modern science and critical historical studies were just beginning to emerge.

Unfortunately, modern skeptics still refer to the condemnation of Galileo to prove that the Catholic Church is against science and out of touch with reality and the modern world. However, noted Hungarian historian of science Father Stanley Jaki has observed that modern science and technology *only* emerged spontaneously in Western society, which was Christian. Far from being opposed to science, Christianity gave birth to science because of its respect for the human intellect and its desire to promote the spread of the gospel through every legitimate means, such as the development of the modern science of navigation. Jaki also gives examples of leading Catholic clergymen who had made scientific discoveries based on observation and reason two or three centuries before the secular scientists of the Enlightenment.

Even apart from this, the Catholic Church has long recognized two important limitations of reason and science that are often neglected, even today. First, the secular philosophers and scientists who optimistically exalted the capabilities of reason frequently denied or overlooked the reality of original sin. The doctrine of original sin points out that man's reason is darkened, to some extent, by sin and selfishness. Reason is only used by human beings, who have prejudices and presuppositions that are influenced by original and personal sin and who, therefore, are not perfectly objective or unbiased as is often claimed. Only God's grace and the light of Christian faith can enable our reason to see the truth clearly and to function in full accord with God's plan.

Second, reason and science may be able to tell us what reality *is*, but it is beyond the scope of reason and the sciences to tell us the ultimate goal, purpose or meaning of their observations and discoveries. They can tell us what reality *is* but not what it's all *about*, its goal. Scientific discoveries, for example, have been used to accomplish great good, such as in medicine, but they have also brought the whole human race to the brink of destruction through the nuclear arms race. Only Christianity can provide the full picture of what life is ultimately about and how the advances of reason and science can be used purely for human good.

During this period from 1650 to 1789, the Catholic Church was only beginning to formulate these ideas. They took time to emerge. Rather than allow reason and the findings of science to receive unqualified acceptance, it is true that the Catholic Church sometimes condemned or cautioned against certain propositions of philosophers and scientists that were later found to be correct. It is part of the wisdom of the Catholic Church to move slowly before accepting a new thing.

It is easier to remove a caution against or a condemnation of something than it is to stop or to condemn something that has already gained wide popularity or acceptance in the Church and in society. The papal condemnation of Galileo's findings does not appear to have impeded the progress of modern astronomy or science in the long run, and some of the greatest scientists of the modern age have been faithful Catholics. The same cannot be said of the effect of Enlightenment rationalism's criticisms of religion.

3. *The Quest for a True Catholic Spirituality.*

In France there were two movements in the seventeenth century that indicate people were searching for a true Catholic spirituality for their times. These two movements also reflect the confusion of the times, however, because both were eventually condemned by the Catholic Church because of certain errors.

Jansenism was a spiritual movement in France led by a few priests, a layman and a convent of religious sisters at Port-Royal near Paris. The movement was named after Cornelius Jansen, a bishop of Ypres, Holland (d. 1638). Jansen had written so strongly about the absolute corruption of human nature by original sin that in 1653 Pope Innocent X condemned a number of propositions of his writing that were Calvinistic.

Jansen's supporters in France, however, thought that Jansen had been falsely accused. They said that the real problem was that the Catholic Church, especially in France, had grown lukewarm and lax in its view of sin; Jansen had not been too strict. They pointed to the way the Jesuits approached the forgiveness of sin in the sacrament of penance to illustrate their point. The Jesuits, the Jansenists said, were not calling people to repentance, because they were too concerned not to offend people and were always considering the special situation of each particular case that might lessen the person's guilt. The study of such cases developed into a "science" called *casuistry*.

There was some substance to this criticism, and the Catholic Church did require a stronger call to repentance in the confessional. However, the Jansenists also had a problem in setting too high an ideal of perfectionism and austerity in the Christian life, which they wanted to set as a standard for all Catholics. The Jansenists, throughout the dispute, were not very submissive to the decisions and authority of the pope or the French bishops; and it was not until 1713 that the Jansenist cause was finally put to rest.

Today Jansenism can recur as a tendency toward an excessive sense of guilt and sin that is the result of scrupulosity or an overly severe conscience. However, most Catholics today generally need to be more wary of the other extreme—a permissive conscience that does not recognize the horror and seriousness of sin and the constant need for genuine repentance and continual conversion to Christ.

Another heresy that emerged in the French Church during this period was Quietism. Originating in the writings of Spaniard Miguel de Molinos, Quietism was a type of spirituality that advocated total passivity before God in prayer. According to this theory, God must be allowed to do everything in prayer, so the mind must be purged of all images. People were supposed to be so detached from themselves before God that they even lost all concern for their own salvation. The Jesuits, who advocated meditation (the active cooperation of the mind and imagination in prayer), spoke out against this teaching. Quietism was finally condemned by the pope because it did not allow for necessary human cooperation with God's action and grace and because it denied that Christians should desire their own salvation.

It should be evident from these last two topics that there was some confusion about proper Catholic spirituality, especially in France. It is true that this confusion existed among some Catholics, but a broader and more positive view of the situation is given by Alfred Lapple in his book *The Catholic Church: A Brief History:*

> *While rationalism was making inroads into theology and preaching, there was also an upsurge in religious life, with the practice of eucharistic adoration, devotions to the Child Jesus, the Sacred Heart, and Mary, the nuptial mysticism practiced in many convents, the Jesuit theater, plays for Christmas, the Passion, and Easter, and the popular hymns that served as a catechetical accompaniment to the liturgical year. After the papacy had won new respect through the Council of Trent and the slowly implemented process of pastoral reform, an alliance developed between the Vatican and the "little people." The progressive ideas of reformed Catholicism, with its anti-papal mentality, got nowhere with simple believers who clung to the veneration of the saints, to splendid Corpus Christi processions and pilgrimages, and to exposition of the Blessed Sacrament on altars ablaze with candles. Such fidelity to the Church was marked, on the one hand, by concern for tradition and, on the other, by feast days and ceremonies in which the pious heart could thrill and catch a glimpse of heaven while still on earth.*[2]

Even in a modern world in which Christianity and the Catholic Church seemingly were becoming foreign elements, the average person who was not a philosopher or scientist could still feel at home with the normal life of prayer and devotion within the Catholic Church. The spiritual vibrancy of the Catholic Church is also evidenced in this period by the founding of three important religious orders of men: the monastic Trappist order in 1664, the missionary and renewal-oriented Passionist order (1725) and the Redemptorists (1732).

4. *The Catholic Church and the State.*

The Catholic Church appeared outwardly strong and influential in the eighteenth century, but inwardly the flames of renewed vigor from the Catholic Reformation had largely died away by 1650, and the internal weaknesses caused by the Enlightenment and the rise of nationalism began to manifest themselves in this century. Rulers of the traditional Catholic nations—France, Spain and Austria—attempted to usurp more authority from the pope and the Catholic Church and sometimes succeeded.

In France the movement called Gallicanism was actually an attempt to create a French national Catholic Church in which the pope had no real authority and the king really ruled. King Louis XIV, an absolute monarch, directed the passage of Four (Gallican) Articles in 1682, which virtually denied the pope any authority in France. Pope Innocent VI (d. 1689) stood up to Louis until his own death, causing the king to strike a compromise with the succeeding pope. In Germany a similar attempt was made to control the churches.

The Bourbon and Habsburg families, rulers of France, Spain and Austria, had negotiated concordats with the popes, giving these secular rulers the right to nominate their own bishops and to prohibit the publication of papal decrees. These families even gained the influence to see that the office of pope was held by weaker, compromise candidates through most of the eighteenth century, with the exception of Benedict XIV (1740–1758). When Pope Pius VI (1775–1799) visited the Austrian emperor Joseph II (1765–1790) in 1782 to prevent further restrictions on the Catholic Church there, he was sent away by the emperor without achieving his goal. Joseph, an Enlightenment rationalist, dissolved the monasteries and convents throughout his empire because they had no practical use. Pius VII (1800–1823) looked on helplessly as Napoleon crowned himself Holy Roman Emperor in 1804. The papacy had diminished in power since the Middle Ages, when the popes dictated policy to emperors as well as crowned them.

Perhaps the saddest example of papal weakness and the troubled condition of the Catholic Church at the end of the eighteenth century was the suppression of the Jesuit order by Pope Clement XIV in 1773. The Jesuits, who were known for their personal loyalty to the pope, had been under much pressure and attack throughout the eighteenth century. They took a traditional theological stand against the Enlightenment, which made them enemies of intellectuals. Their missionary methods in the Far East, which entailed adapting Catholicism to the existing culture, had been investigated beginning in 1633 and finally condemned by popes in 1715 and 1742. Their founding of Christian villages for the natives in Paraguay, South America, was attacked by the Spanish and Portuguese governments for political reasons. Finally, a trade enterprise with the New World run by a French Jesuit priest collapsed, and the Jesuit order was suppressed in France in 1764 to pay off the debt.

Under pressure from all sides, Pope Clement suppressed the Jesuit order, which resulted in the closing of six hundred religious houses and hundreds of schools and the dispersion of more than twenty thousand Jesuit priests and brothers. The Jesuit order, which had been the vanguard of the Catholic Reformation and a leader of the Catholic missionary effort throughout the world, was then extinct, except in Russia, where Catherine the Great refused to implement the papal mandate.

Catholic life went on, but during the eighteenth century the prestige and influence of the Church reached a low point. The Protestant churches began to take the lead in world missionary expansion (which also had to do with the decline of Spain, Portugal and France as world powers). The challenges of the philosophers of the Enlightenment had not yet been adequately answered by Catholic theologians, and there was again a need for renewal and reform in Catholic religious orders. As if this were not enough, the Catholic Church in France, which had been faced by the challenges of Gallicanism, Jansenism, Quietism and the suppression of the Jesuits, was now about to experience its greatest test, the French Revolution.

THE FRENCH REVOLUTION

The French Revolution was, in many ways, the climax of the Enlightenment. Due to a financial crisis in France, a general assembly was called in which the common people (the Third Estate) overthrew King Louis XVI and formed a revolutionary government. The clergy of France (the First Estate) had supported this revolution and at first enjoyed the favor of the new government. In 1790, however, the new rulers of France demanded that all priests and bishops swear an unconditional oath of allegiance to the new regime or lose their office. This Civil Constitution of the Clergy was an undisguised attack on the freedom of the Catholic Church and the authority of the pope.

The pope remained silent for eight months, while about half the clergy took the oath—hoping that it wouldn't affect much in practice—and half refused out of loyalty to the Church. This division brought confusion and turmoil to the Catholic Church in France, especially when, in 1792, the thirty or forty thousand priests who had refused to take the oath were driven into hiding or exile; many were later killed when the French Revolution became more radical in 1793.

The next step of the revolution began in 1793, when the government took steps to dechristianize France and set up a new religion. All Christian holidays, including Sunday, were suppressed, and Catholic churches were turned into Temples of Reason. A statue of the Goddess of Reason was set up in Notre Dame Cathedral in Paris. Later the government decided that this religion of reason was too close to atheism, so Robespierre began his Cult of the Supreme Being, which professed belief in God but had no dogmas. Deism became the official religion of France, a traditionally Catholic country.

The true faith of the people could not be suppressed, however. After the novelty of these new religions wore off, the government decided to allow freedom of religion in 1795, and there was a rush to open the Catholic churches.

When Napoleon took over the throne of France in 1796, he had to deal with the pope. Pope Pius VI died when Napoleon took him prisoner, but the new pope, Pius VII (1800–1823), was a strong leader who stood up to Napoleon and refused to compromise the rights of the Catholic Church. Napoleon and Pius VII signed a concordat in 1801 that reestablished the Catholic Church in France and ended the split between the clergy who had sworn the government oath and those who had refused. Napoleon still attempted to control the Catholic Church and the pope, but Pius VII showed his strength by refusing to bend to Napoleon's will, even when Napoleon arrested the pope and kept him a prisoner in France for six years (1808–1814). Under political pressure Napoleon released the pope, who returned to Rome amid shouts of joy and victory. Napoleon was soon overthrown and exiled to Elba, while the Catholic Church in France was restored and the pope's authority reaffirmed.

What are the lessons and results of the French Revolution? First, it demonstrates the influence of the Enlightenment. It is shocking that a country that had been Catholic for more than one thousand years could be turned overnight into an atheistic or deistic land. However, the French Revolution also shows how superficial the Enlightenment really was. Some philosophers or radicals might have believed in the "Religion of Reason," but the common people never abandoned their Catholic faith and joyfully returned to it.

Second, the Enlightenment did leave some bitter scars on the French Church that are evident in France and throughout Europe even today. There arose a bitter anticlericalism—sentiment against the clergy—that remained as a result of their division. Secularization and a secular, or "this worldly," spirit began to spread in France and elsewhere. In France the introduction of civil divorce, civil marriage and the secular (public) school system were visible expressions of this.

Third, the prestige and authority of the pope began to be restored. Pope Pius VII's heroic stand against Napoleon won the admiration of people everywhere. In an age in which society and governments were in flux and turmoil, Catholics began to look to the pope more and more for inspiration, strength and guidance. This strong emphasis on the authority and leadership of the pope came to be called *ultramontanism*. This emphasis continued in the Catholic Church in the nineteenth century.

THE NINETEENTH CENTURY AND POLITICAL LIBERALISM

Because of the disastrous failure of the French Revolution, most of the nations of Europe took strong measures to prevent similar occurrences in the first thirty years of the nineteenth century. The Bourbon kings were restored in France, and strong, absolute rulers were established elsewhere in Europe. In reality this was the final stage of a form of government and society that was passing away. The age of kings and absolute rulers was soon to be replaced in Europe, as it had been in the newly formed United States of America, with representative governments that allowed for more political participation and freedom of expression in different areas. This meant that the alliance of Church and state that had existed in Europe since the time of Constantine was about to come to an end.

The most important question for the Catholic Church in the nineteenth century concerned its attitude toward the great changes occurring in society. *Liberalism* is a general term used for the movement favoring change and the establishment of a new order. Liberalism in politics supported constitutional or representative governments (instead of monarchies), religious toleration, the separation of church and state and freedom of the press and education. Those Catholics opposed to political liberalism feared a recurrence of the anarchy and chaos of the French Revolution and the suppression of the Church. They also strongly objected to freedom of conscience, of the press and of education on the grounds that false ideas and beliefs would then be put on the same level as the truth.

These more conservative or "integralist" Catholics wanted to maintain the alliance of the Catholic Church with the state so that only Catholic truth would be advocated and upheld by the government. A "free market" of ideas, in which truth and error were put on the same plane, held no appeal for them.

At first only a few Catholics supported political liberalism, since it was so radically different than the way society had operated for centuries. In 1830 French priest Félicité de Lamenais (1782–1854) began to advocate political liberties as a way of freeing the Catholic Church from political ties and of enabling it to pursue its spiritual mission. Lamenais was a prophet ahead of his time though. When he went to Rome to seek support for his position, Pope Gregory XVI (pope from 1831 to 1846) instead firmly condemned political liberalism in *Mirari Vos* (1832). In the pope's view, liberalism was allied with the skeptical philosophy of the Enlightenment, and he had experienced trouble with liberal political revolutionaries in the Papal States.

A number of successful revolutions creating constitutional governments occurred in Europe (Belgium) and South America around 1830, and so by the time Pius IX (1814–1878) became pope in 1846, he was more favorable to the forces advocating political freedom. Some Catholics and secular rulers were shocked that a liberal had become pope. However, when some revolutionaries killed the archbishop of Paris and others drove the newly elected pope out of Italy soon after his election, Pius IX decided that political liberalism was dangerous to the Church and to society and took a strong stand against it. When French troops enabled Pius IX to return to Rome in 1850, he began a long struggle against the political forces advocating constitutional governments and political freedoms. It was only by military force that the Papal States of central Italy were seized from control of Pius IX in 1870, thus ending the long history of the Catholic Church as a political force in Europe.

What was a tragedy in the eyes of the pope and many Catholics—the loss of the Papal States and the rise of liberal constitutional governments—turned out to be a blessing and an opportunity for the Catholic Church. As Lamenais had predicted, when the political alliance between the Church and state was ended, the Catholic Church was able to focus more clearly on its spiritual mission. Throughout Europe the Catholic Church lost thousands of acres of land and countless monasteries and other houses through the secularization (government takeover) of Church property in the nineteenth century. The new governmental system, in general, did lead to a financially poorer and politically less powerful Catholic Church. Far from destroying the Church, though, this resulted in the Catholic Church's focusing on its spiritual identity and mission.

THE CATHOLIC CHURCH AND
INTELLECTUAL LIBERALISM

In England and Germany in the nineteenth century, a group of Catholics appeared who could be called intellectual liberals. They desired that the Catholic faith be examined and presented in light of modern philosophy, scientific advances and new methods of historical study. Some Catholic scholars at the University of Tübingen in Germany sought to renew Catholic theology in this spirit. They looked upon the Church and Church doctrine not as static and unchanging but as alive, dynamic and developing—like the human body.

A few of these men, such as Johann A. Möhler (1796–1838) and Friedrich von Schlegel (d. 1829), were to have a positive influence on Catholic theology in the twentieth century. In England Lord John Acton and John Henry Newman—who became a Catholic after being a leader of the Oxford Movement, a renewal of Anglicanism—shared a desire for a new approach to Catholic theology that emphasized the development of Catholic tradition and openness to new avenues of Catholic thought.

The popes and other leaders of the Catholic Church were understandably cautious about this new approach to Catholic theology. They were afraid that it could be tainted by the rationalism and skepticism of the Enlightenment and could actually undermine the Catholic faith. In fact, Pope Pius IX was so concerned about the false ideas that he saw infiltrating the Catholic Church that in 1864 he published a Syllabus of Errors of the modern world. He saw the Catholic people in confusion because of the conflicting political, economic, social and religious ideas widespread in European society as a result of the new freedom of thought, and he sensed his deep responsibility as the pope to teach God's people with clarity.

Unfortunately, the Syllabus of Errors condemned most of the new ideas of the day and gave the impression that the Catholic Church was against everything in the modern world. Indeed, the last statement in the Syllabus rejected and condemned the belief that the Catholic Church should reconcile herself with "progress, liberalism, and modern civilization." Although numerous Catholic leaders were quick to explain that this was *not* a condemnation of everything new and modern, many people got that impression. The Catholic Church looked as if it was becoming a fortress church, standing in opposition to the modern world and rejecting all new ideas.

POPE PIUS IX AND
THE FIRST VATICAN COUNCIL

In his condemnation of modern errors, Pope Pius IX was reminding Catholics that they should look to the Church of Christ for guidance for their lives and for truth and not to the modern world. He realized that the society at large, since it was no longer guided by the spiritual authority of the Catholic Church, was becoming an open forum of opinions, good and bad. The pope wanted people to remember that God's revelation of the truth was given assuredly to the *Church*, not to public opinion or to the new ideas of scholars.

Pius IX sought to clarify certain points of the Catholic faith that were being questioned or disputed. For example, he formally defined as a doctrine of faith in 1854 that Mary, the

Mother of God, was conceived without original sin, the doctrine of the Immaculate Conception. This dogma was miraculously confirmed when Mary herself appeared to Bernadette Soubirous in Lourdes, France, in 1858 and announced to her, "I am the Immaculate Conception." Even though Catholics are not bound to believe in the appearances of Mary, most Catholics look upon the thousands of healings that have occurred through the waters of Lourdes as confirmation of its authenticity.

At the First Vatican Council in Rome in 1869, Pope Pius IX called the Catholic bishops together to discuss the issue of the relationship between faith and reason and the question of the primacy (governing authority) and teaching infallibility of the pope. This council passed two constitutions. *Dei Filius* spoke of the ultimate authority of God's revelation and taught that nature and reason are subordinate to grace and faith. This was an important response to the Enlightenment view that reason is superior to faith.

The second constitution, *Pastor Aeternus*, on the primacy and infallibility of the pope, was more controversial. Although Catholics had actually believed in these two concepts for centuries, some bishops thought that it would further divide the Church from the world to define these things at that time. The vast majority of bishops, however, voted for the constitution. They knew that the leadership and teaching authority of the pope had been an essential source of guidance for the Church in troubled and confused times in the past and was especially needed in the modern world, in which papal authority was under attack.

This constitution taught that when the pope speaks *ex cathedra* (literally, "from the chair" of Peter), that is, speaking in his office of chief shepherd of the Church and as the successor of Saint Peter, he is granted by the Holy Spirit the gift of infallible truth when he formally defines a doctrine concerning faith or morals. This does *not*, of course, mean that whatever the pope says is infallible, although Catholics presume that even the ordinary teaching of a pope is true and valuable.

The outbreak of the Franco-Prussian War in 1870 brought the First Vatican Council to an abrupt end. It was halted before the bishops could discuss their own role in the Church and the role of laypeople and religious. As a result, the Catholic Church from 1870 until Vatican II put a very heavy emphasis on the office and authority of the pope, in the absence of a strong balancing statement about bishops, priests and laypeople. The office of the pope had gone from a position of extreme weakness and lack of spiritual authority at the end of the eighteenth century to a position of great spiritual and moral authority by the middle of the nineteenth century. Pope Pius IX, who had the longest rule of any pope in history, had much to do with bringing this about.

SPIRITUAL ADVANCES
IN THE NINETEENTH CENTURY

Perhaps Pius IX's greatest achievement was to deepen and renew the spiritual life of Catholics. He encouraged frequent reception of the sacraments and devotion to Mary and the Sacred Heart of Jesus, and above all he stressed the centrality of Jesus Christ—true God and true man. Pius realized that the best answer to the rationalistic tendencies of the Enlightenment was to stress that Christianity is a religion of the heart as well as the head. He helped people rediscover the sacramental nature of Catholic life and the reality of the supernatural.

Earlier in the century, in 1814, Pope Pius VII had reestablished the Society of Jesus, the Jesuits, which attracted young men by the thousands. Other new religious orders began, such as the Marianists, Marists, Christian Brothers, Sisters of Charity of Saint Joseph (founded by Saint Elizabeth Ann Seton in 1809), Sisters of Loretto, Paulists (founded by Isaac Hecker), Salesians, Society of the Divine Word and White Fathers. These orders engaged in a wide variety of pastoral and social ministries, education and missionary work. New and revitalized religious orders were, once again, a key to the renewal of the whole Catholic Church. The Society of Foreign Missions was reestablished in 1815, and with the help of the Jesuits, the missionary activity of the Catholic Church was revitalized. The Jesuits doubled their membership during the papacy of Pius IX, and the seminaries and monasteries of all orders were filled with new recruits.

Whatever criticism is made of Pius IX's attitude toward the modern world must be seen in the light of the great renewal of Catholic faith and life that resulted from his policies. This century was not only an age of challenges but also of reawakening of the Catholic faith, led not only by popes but by great saints as well. Saint John Vianney (1786–1859), the Curé of Ars, was a gifted pastor who was able to read people's hearts. Saint Clement Hofbauer was a Redemptorist who revived the Church in southern Germany.

John Carroll became the first Catholic bishop in the United States, appointed in 1789 by Pope Pius VI to serve the diocese of Baltimore. During the first half of the nineteenth century, the Catholic Church grew from a mere 3 percent of the U.S. population to the largest single Christian body in the country, largely through emigration from Catholic countries of Europe. Even though the Catholic Church in the United States was persecuted and ostracized and spent most of its energies in establishing itself and defending its rights, it also produced some notable saints: John Neumann, Elizabeth Seton, Frances Cabrini and Native American Blessed Kateri Tekakwitha.

POPE LEO XIII

The successor of Pope Pius IX, Leo XIII (1878–1903), sought to restore the leadership of the papacy and the influence of the Catholic Church in the eyes of the modern world. Though not a liberal, Leo XIII was a diplomat who realized that the only way to prevent the Catholic Church from appearing as a foreign element in the modern world was to seek conciliation with modern society and learning.

Pope Leo XIII took a number of steps in this direction. First he made John Henry Newman, author of *On the Development of Christian Doctrine* and *The Grammar of Assent*, a cardinal. Newman had previously been suspected of being a dangerous liberal. Pope Leo knew that giving honor to Newman would also promote the Catholic Church in England.

Second, Leo strove hard to act as a friend of democracy and the new constitutional governments instead of only denouncing their errors. Third, he opened the Vatican archives to researchers, which seemed to be encouraging Catholics to pursue historical studies and to blend Catholic theology with biblical criticism.

Fourth, one of Pope Leo XIII's outstanding contributions was to take a stand on the social and economic issues of the day. In his encyclical *Rerum Novarum* (1891), Pope Leo defended justice and better working conditions for workers, indicating that Catholics should take an active role in providing constructive solutions for the problems and injustice brought about by the Industrial Revolution. *Rerum Novarum* is the first in a line of great Catholic social encyclicals.

Fifth, Leo XIII revived Catholic devotion to the Holy Spirit, calling all churches to observe the novena of Pentecost to pray for the grace of the Holy Spirit, dedicating the new century to the Holy Spirit's work and publishing an encyclical letter on the Holy Spirit, *Divinum Illud Munus*, in 1897.

In two areas Pope Leo XIII found it necessary to support more traditional Catholic teaching and life. In 1879 he declared the theology of Saint Thomas Aquinas (1225–1274) to be standard for judging all Catholic theology and philosophy. This gave impetus to the development of Neo-Thomism and Neo-Scholasticism, revivals of the thought of Saint Thomas Aquinas and of the medieval universities. Especially in the seminaries, the theology of Saint Thomas was the official theology of the Catholic Church right up to the Second Vatican Council and still is widely respected today.

Pope Leo also had to impose discipline on some teachers and movements that were drawing false or potentially dangerous conclusions from their use of modern methods of biblical and historical studies. Father Alfred Loisy was removed from professorship at the University of Paris in 1893; in the same year Pope Leo XIII promulgated the encyclical letter *Providentissimus Deus* that affirmed the complete inerrancy of the Bible, defending it from rationalistic interpretations. In 1899 he also condemned a heresy called Americanism, which saw active and human virtues as more valuable than supernatural virtues, such as humility and charity.

Leo XIII succeeded in pursuing a careful path of reconciling the Catholic Church to the modern world and dealing creatively with its new challenges. He encouraged new approaches to scholarship and theology while reaffirming the value of traditional Catholic theology and guarding against modern errors. Depending on the strength of God and helped by the renewed influence of the office of pope, especially among Catholics, Leo XIII led the Catholic Church boldly out of a century of confusion and renewal and into the twentieth century.

the CATHOLIC CHURCH
in the TWENTIETH CENTURY
(AD 1900–1963)

Sometimes we tend to think of our own times as the best or most advanced because we have gone beyond what was achieved in times before. There is especially a temptation to exalt the twentieth century because of the technological advances and the progress in science that were achieved. In 1900 automobiles were novelties owned only by a few; airplanes and television did not exist; and there were few of the modern conveniences, like telephone service, that many people enjoy today. Space travel, atomic weapons and nearly instantaneous worldwide communications would be considered science fiction.

From a Christian point of view, the twentieth century must be evaluated differently. In 1850 Christians comprised about one-half of the world's population. By 1950 this figure had shrunk to one-third. One important factor in the decline of the number of Christians was the rise of communism and other atheistic forms of government in the twentieth century. This contributed to the twentieth century's being the greatest age of Christian martyrs since the early Church. In fact, far more Christians were put to death for their faith in this century than in any other. The emphasis of the Second Vatican Council on the Church's active role in the modern world and the calls of Popes Paul VI and John Paul II for a renewed effort to evangelize the world were timely and essential.

Within the segment of the world that was free to exercise Christian faith, secular humanism (a product of the Enlightenment) and individualistic materialism (selfish pursuit of money and possessions) sapped the strength and vigor of Christianity. Many Christians held to the outward form of their faith without personal knowledge of God or the power of the Holy Spirit. Many Christians in European and North American societies threw off the mask of external religious conformity and simply ceased participating in the worship and life of the Church. Few young people were found at the worship services of many Western churches, giving rise to the fear that a whole generation might be lost to Christ.

Meanwhile, mankind continued to search for hope and meaning in the century in which two world wars killed more people within fifty years than have died in all the previous wars in human history, not to mention the threat of nuclear annihilation.

These facts are not presented to shock or disturb but to have us look at the twentieth century with a sober realism about where the world and Christianity stood as that century closed. The twentieth century also may be called an age of ideologies. Since Christianity was rejected by much of the Western world as the unifying force of society and the source of moral guidance, Western man began seeking a replacement by raising to the status of religion the economic and political ideologies of capitalism, socialism, communism and others.

The twentieth century was a time of great peril and challenge but also a time of great opportunity and hope. Catholics are a people of hope who know that where sin abounds, God's grace abounds even more (see Romans 5:20). It is thus not surprising that the Second Vatican Council turned out to be, in the words of Pope John Paul II, "the great grace bestowed on the Church in the twentieth century."[1]

SAINT PIUS X (1903–1914)

Elected at the dawn of the twentieth century, Pope Pius's major concern was to strengthen Catholic worship and to protect the Catholic Church against modern errors. He called for religious education of youth through the Confraternity of Christian Doctrine (CCD) and moved the age for first receiving the sacraments of reconciliation and the Eucharist to the age of reason (around seven years old). He also encouraged all Catholics to receive Communion at Mass weekly and worked to renew music in the liturgy. His reforms in the area of worship have had a profound influence on Catholic life up to the present day.

Pius X also began the monumental task of gathering the complicated tangle of Church law into a single, unified Code of Canon Law. This was completed and promulgated in 1917. Pius had a concern for bringing the Catholic faith out into the modern world through a movement of laypeople known as Catholic Action. This resulted both in the transformation of society and the conversion of many to the Catholic Church.

Pius X also took a prophetic step with regard to society when he asked the Catholic Church in France to surrender all its property and revenues to the hostile French government rather than submit to its control. The French Church did so and was rewarded by a great spiritual revival.

All these things and more led Pius X to be declared a saint in 1948, the first pope to be canonized since the sixteenth century. Yet many people today only remember Pius X for his decisive action in dealing with a group of Catholic scholars known as the Modernists.

Modernism arose in the nineteenth century among Protestants who examined the Bible using methods of historical and literary criticism. These liberal Protestant scholars did *not* think that the Bible could be properly interpreted through literal reading or even through traditional approaches of interpretation, such as were used by the early fathers of the Church. This approach split Protestantism into two camps: liberal Protestants, who accepted this critical approach to the Bible, and fundamentalist Protestants, who believed that this new approach undermined the authentic meaning of the Bible.

When Catholics such as a French priest, Alfred Loisy (1857–1940), English Jesuit George Tyrrell (d. 1909) and others started using these same methods of scholarship (even to refute the false conclusions of the liberal Protestants), the popes, beginning with Leo XIII, were very wary. Would the same forces that were dividing Protestantism now cause division and confusion in the Catholic Church? Pope Pius X was determined that this would not occur. The Catholic Modernists could not be allowed to teach the simple faithful that Jesus was only a prophet who was unique because of his consciousness of

God but actually had no clear notion of his own divinity, or that Jesus had no specific intention to establish the sacraments or to found a Church. The Modernists seemed to be advocating a position that called into question or rejected many of the basic Catholic dogmas about Christ and the Church.

However honorable their motives or intelligent their methods, Pius X considered their conclusions and was convinced that the Catholic Modernists must be stopped quickly and decisively. In 1907 *Lamentabili Sane*, a list of condemned Modernist propositions, was published, followed shortly by a full-scale encyclical against Modernism, *Pascendi Dominici Gregis*. In 1910 all Catholic clergy and pastors were required to swear an oath to reject all Modernist teaching. Pope Pius X even instituted a secret police to insure that Modernism was not taught in Catholic seminaries and universities.

Pius X may have overreacted to the threat of Modernism, which led to the stifling of creative Catholic research, especially in the areas of biblical and historical studies, over the next fifty years. From the long-range perspective, however, it appears that Pius X was wise in making sure that Catholics would not too rashly adopt a new approach to the Bible and to the emergence of the Church, since these are the very foundations of Christianity and Catholicism. The Catholic Church has benefited, in the long run, by taking so many years before engaging in unrestricted research in these delicate areas.

POPE BENEDICT XV (1914–1922)

The story of the Catholic Church during the papacy of Benedict XV was inseparably bound up with the great conflagration that swept Europe during this period: the Great War, World War I. Pope Benedict maintained a strict political neutrality and vigorously condemned abuses on either side, publicly or privately, whenever he perceived them. Three of his major encyclicals dealt with peace and reconciliation. The pope also personally authorized alms for the relief of war victims: five and a half million *lire* from his own pocket and thirty million from collections from the Catholic Church at large. Although Benedict XV was sometimes suspected and criticized by the nations involved in the war because he refused to side with their cause, ultimately he did more than any world agency to break down the barriers of hatred.

A remarkable event that provided both warning and hope to the world occurred during Benedict's papacy. In 1917 Mary, the Mother of God, reportedly appeared to three children in Fatima, Portugal, on the thirteenth day of six consecutive months. Mary predicted the end of World War I but also warned that unless special prayer and eucharistic reparation were offered, "Russia will spread her errors through the world, promoting wars and the persecution of the Church."[2] This was a strange prophecy, since Russia was then a weak, agrarian nation suffering the internal throes of civil war.

Each time the Mother of God appeared, she asked that the rosary be prayed daily, with proper meditation on the Word of God as contained in the mysteries of the rosary. Finally Mary asked that individuals, families and nations (Russia in particular) be consecrated to the Immaculate Heart of Mary. The consecration of Russia was to be carried out by the pope in union with the bishops of the world.

It is important to note that the heart of the message of Fatima was the basic gospel message—calling God's people to repentance, faith in Jesus Christ and the authentic living of Christianity day by day. To demonstrate to the world the authenticity of her visitations at Fatima, Mary told the children that on October 13, 1917, God would provide a sign. On that day one hundred thousand onlookers, both Christians and skeptics, witnessed the sun appearing to whirl and dance in the sky, a phenomenon that no one has ever been able to explain scientifically.

Another event changed the history of the world. The October Revolution in Russia brought the Bolshevik party of Lenin to power, marking the beginning of the communist rule of Russia: the birth of the Union of Soviet Socialist Republics. Communism is an atheistic political philosophy developed by Karl Marx (1818–1883) that calls for the overthrow of oppressive capitalist governments by the proletariat, or working class, who will henceforth control the means of production and govern themselves. In practice communist countries turn out to be dictatorships ruled by a few.

Marx rejected all religion as an "opiate of the masses" that teaches people to seek their reward in heaven while accepting oppression and suffering in this world. For Marx and communism, this world is all there is, and so religion has no place. In particular, the Catholic Church, with its worldwide fellowship and obedience to the pope, was recognized by Marxists as a chief enemy.

Although the Catholic Church did not begin to strongly denounce communism until its effects began to be felt, as early as 1878 Pope Leo XIII foresaw the danger of communism when he called Marx's theory "the fatal plague which insinuates itself into the marrow of human society, only to bring about its ruin."[3] The message of Fatima was that the only way communism would ultimately be defeated was through the prayer of Christians, not by military might.

POPE PIUS XI (1922–1939)

After writing nine official documents on the threat of communism, Pope Pius XI scathingly condemned atheistic communism in his encyclical letter *Divini Redemptoris*, issued on the feast of Saint Joseph the Worker in 1937. Pius XI also faced the challenge of two other dangerous modern ideologies during his papacy—Fascism and Nazism, both manifesting themselves in the form of repressive, totalitarian governments.

In 1922 Benito Mussolini led a Fascist takeover of Italy. Realizing that he needed the support of the Catholic Church in Italy, Mussolini signed a treaty with Pius XI in 1929, which brought peace between the government and the Church but only after Pius XI surrendered the Papal States to Mussolini's control. This was a great blessing to the Church, since it marked the end of the idea that the pope's authority depended on possessing an earthly kingdom. The pope renounced all official Catholic support of the Fascist government and accepted only independence and the safety of 109 acres of land, Vatican City, in return.

In 1933 Pius XI also negotiated a concordat with the new Nazi leader of Germany, Adolf Hitler. Again the pope renounced any political role for the Catholic Church in Hitler's regime and only sought to secure the full freedom and rights of Catholics in Germany. Before the ink was dry on his treaty, Hitler began to repress the Catholic Church and enact his abominable policies against the Jews. The Fascists followed a similar course in Italy. After a few years of patient and futile protests, Pope Pius XI issued his fiery encyclical *Mit Brennender Sorge* in 1937, which outrightly condemned Fascism and Nazism.

The Catholic Church suffered also through civil war in Spain in 1936 and governments that attempted to stamp out Catholicism in Russia and Mexico. Priests and bishops in both Russia and Mexico were imprisoned or put to death by the communist regimes. The Catholic Church suffered tremendous repression in Mexico for most of the twentieth century. These were tragic events, especially for a pope whose principal aim had been to establish the reign and peace of Christ in society. Pius's institution of the Feast of Christ the King in 1925, to remind the world of Christ's kingship over nations, was necessary but fatally ignored in many places.

Pope Pius XI also provided leadership for the Catholic Church's missionary activity and social teaching. The missionary activity of the Catholic Church continued to expand throughout the world, and Pius XI was the first pope to consecrate bishops from among the native peoples in large numbers.

On the fortieth anniversary of Leo XIII's great social encyclical *(Rerum Novarum)*, Pius XI published his own encyclical (*Quadrigesimo Anno*, 1931) in which he presented a serious moral analysis of the questions of capital and labor and of the merits and limitations of socialism and capitalism. As always in Catholic social teaching, the values of Jesus Christ and his gospel were taken as the highest standard to evaluate and judge all political and economic theories and systems. Pius XI continued to encourage Catholic Action as a way of permeating the world with the values of the gospel and to emphasize that the only way to peace and happiness is through the reign of Christ the King over all of human life.

POPE PIUS XII (1939–1958)

Pope Pius XII, who had been the Vatican secretary of state under Pius XI, was chosen as pope largely because of his diplomatic ability and holiness. Both of these qualities were desperately needed, as the world was plunged into war by Adolf Hitler and his Nazi regime shortly after Pius's election. Pius's policy was to maintain an appearance of neutrality. This was wise, since the Vatican was located in the middle of the Axis (German-Italian) bloc.

In reality Pius was deeply opposed to both communism and Nazi-Fascism, though he loved the German people and culture. Instead of denouncing Nazism in a strong, public way, as Pius XI had done, Pius XII thought that such an approach would just bring on more suffering and reprisals for both Christians and Jews in Germany and the Axis countries. Instead of rhetoric Pius XII used every means available to provide relief and refuge for the Jews and other persecuted people.

Pinchas Lapide, a Jewish scholar and former Israeli consul to Italy, credits the pope and the Catholic Church with saving some four hundred thousand Jews from certain death. Lapide writes in the book *The Last Three Popes and the Jews*: "The Catholic church saved more Jewish lives during the war than all the other churches, religious institutions and rescue organizations put together. Its record stands in startling contrast to the achievements of the Red Cross and the Western democracies. The Holy See, the nuncios and the entire Catholic Church saved some 400,000 Jews from certain death."[4]

Heinrich Himmler, head of the Nazi secret police, wrote a letter to a subordinate in which he said, "We should not forget that in the long run, the pope in Rome is a greater enemy of National Socialism [the Nazi party] than Churchill or Roosevelt."

Pius XII did speak out against Nazism at times. After his Christmas radio address to the world in 1942, a Nazi leader commented on Pius XII's words: "God, he says, regards all peoples and races as worthy of the same consideration. Here he is clearly speaking on behalf of the Jews. He is virtually accusing the German people of injustice towards the Jews, and makes himself the mouthpiece of the Jewish war criminals."[5]

We also recall the witness of many Christians who stood up against Nazi policies, many of whom sacrificed their lives. One Polish man was saved from death by the heroic self-sacrifice of Franciscan priest Saint Maximilian Kolbe, who freely volunteered to accept death in a starvation bunker in place of a man with a family.

PIUS XII, COMMUNISM AND MARY

Despite the immediate threat of Nazism, Pius XII firmly believed that the greatest modern threat to God's people and humanity was communism. After World War II he aligned the Catholic Church more and more with Western democracies and tried to mobilize world opinion against the communists.

In 1949 he issued a decree that pronounced excommunication on all Catholics belonging to the Communist party.

Pius XII's rejection of communism was certainly related to the appearance of Our Lady at Fatima, who warned of Russia's spreading her errors throughout the world. In 1942 Pius consecrated the world to the Immaculate Heart of Mary, and in 1952 he made a particular consecration of the people of Russia to her Immaculate Heart. He also declared Mary "Queen of the World." All of these acts were in recognition of Mary's special role as intercessor and mother of Christians.

In 1950 Pius XII declared as an infallible doctrine that at the end of her earthly life, Mary was taken up or "assumed," body and soul, into heaven—the dogma of the Assumption. This doctrine had always been believed by the Catholic Church and had been celebrated as a feast day for fifteen hundred years, but the pope wished to define it formally so that it would be a sure sign of hope for all peoples of their own resurrected and glorified bodies, foreshadowed by the assumption of Mary. Since she was conceived and lived without sin, Mary's body was not subject to death and corruption as are the bodies of other human beings, and so she could enter directly into God's glory. Thus Pius XII was known as both a pope of peace and a pope of Mary.

PIUS XII AND MODERN SCHOLARSHIP

Even though Pius XII was much like Pope Leo XIII in equating Thomist theology with authentic Catholic theology, he did begin to open up the fields of biblical and historical scholarship. He warned Catholics against the possible dangers of the new historical theology in his encyclical *Humani Generis* (1950) but allowed Catholic biblical scholars to apply new methods, such as form criticism, in their exegesis through the encyclical *Divino Afflante Spiritu* in 1943.

Also in that year Pius XII published his famous *Mystici Corporis Christi*, which revolutionized the Catholic view of the Church. Instead of looking at the Catholic Church primarily as a human institution or a hierarchy, he encouraged Catholics to view the Church as the mystical body of Christ. This is a concept from Saint Paul's thought that emphasized the mystery and unity of the Church as Christ's body on earth. Pius XII also issued an important encyclical letter on the liturgy, *Mediator Dei*, which anticipated and prepared for the liturgical renewal of Vatican II.

These new approaches to theology began to lift the climate of tension and suspicion that Catholic theologians had worked under since the anti-Modernist oath of 1910. It also paved the way for the blossoming of new forms of Catholic theology, beginning with the Second Vatican Council. There is a long list of Catholic theologians and biblical scholars whose work was made easier through the encouraging attitude of Pius XII.

THE ACHIEVEMENTS OF PIUS XII

Pius XII brought the Catholic Church a new prestige in the world and prepared the Church for the great council of renewal that was soon to come. After the war (1945) many nations sent ambassadors to the Vatican, and the Holy Year of 1950 brought millions of humble pilgrims to Rome. The missionary work of the Catholic Church increased too, as the number of Catholic dioceses worldwide grew from seventeen hundred to more than two thousand. Pius XII made sure that the international character of the Catholic Church was reflected by the appointment of many non-Italian cardinals, who numbered thirty-four (out of fifty-one) at the time of his death.

The Church was now more in touch with the modern world, but it was not until the coming of Pius XII's successor, John XXIII, that a full and open dialogue with the world and a reexamination of the Catholic Church's relationship to it would be achieved.

POPE JOHN XXIII (1958–1963)

Pope Pius XII stood in a line of popes who desired the papacy to be a strong, authoritative force guiding a troubled world. Protestant Christians and others often accused the popes, and Catholics in general, of being triumphalistic, proudly exalting the glory and divine authority of the Catholic Church without acknowledging its human shortcomings and weaknesses. For this reason the Catholic Church was not credible to some who saw that popes and the Catholic Church were human and sinful too.

A pope who changed the entire image of the Catholic Church in the eyes of the world was John XXIII. While previous popes gave the image of being dignified and even a bit aloof, John XXIII was a warm, spontaneous person whose love of life and people was evident. He was also a historian and a veteran ecclesial diplomat who had served in delicate assignments in Eastern Europe and in postwar France.

This seventy-six-year-old pontiff was considered by some to be a pope who would give the papacy a new, pastoral "face" but would not accomplish much because of his temperament and age. Nothing could have been further from the truth. Though he was known as a "people's pope" who walked the streets of Rome, visited hospitals and prisons and often told jokes and stories, it would be incorrect to think of Pope John XXIII as just a simple man.

What is most notable about his brief papacy was his reliance on God and his clear vision. Instead of openly opposing communism or any political system, John XXIII sought reconciliation and addressed his great encyclical letters to all men of good will: *Pacem in Terris* (Peace in the World) and *Mater et Magistra* (On Christianity and Social Progress). He appealed to all peoples to work together to build a better world according to universally recognized norms of justice and the common good.

John XXIII was also a pioneer with regard to the ecumenical movement, the movement for the reunification of all Christians. In the beginning of the nineteenth century, a strong concern for ecumenism arose out of the Protestant missionary movement. Protestants saw how foolish and scandalous it was for different Christian churches to be competing for converts in mission territories. Organizations known as Faith and Order (1925) and Life and Work (1927) endeavored to bring Protestants together on the levels of doctrine and service, respectively. These organizations merged in 1948 to form the World Council of Churches.

The Catholic Church had long stood aloof from active involvement in this ecumenical movement, believing that Protestants should work out their own conflicts before discussing their relationship with the Catholic Church. The attitude of the previous popes was that Jesus established only one true Church and one faith, the Catholic Church and faith. While not denying the uniqueness of the Catholic Church, John XXIII realized Catholics had to reach out to other Christians and get involved with them in order to seek the unity that Jesus desires for his people.

John XXIII had a special place in his heart for the Orthodox Church, since he had served as a papal envoy to the Near East. When the time came for him to call his council, John XXIII invited observers from all Christian traditions and welcomed their input and reflections on the proceedings of the council.

John XXIII was beatified, together with Pius IX, by Pope John Paul II on September 3, 2000.

VATICAN II (1962–1965)

Pope John XXIII shocked the world by calling for a worldwide (ecumenical) council of Catholic bishops in order to promote the unity of all Christians and to bring the Catholic Church up-to-date (*aggiornamento* in Italian) and put it in touch with the needs and concerns of the modern world. Why did he do this? He attributed it simply to an inspiration of the Holy Spirit and asked Catholics to pray for the council: "Renew your wonders in our time, as though for a new Pentecost."[6]

The call for a council was surprising but timely. The technological age had brought much of the world to the brink of a new era, and yet the experience of two world wars and the use of nuclear weapons left deep wounds and confusion about the fate and direction of mankind. How could this ancient Church, which had so long prided itself on resisting changeable trends, survive in a world undergoing such rapid and radical transformation? How was the Catholic Church supposed to understand itself and present itself to such a world? These were the questions with which the pope wished the bishops to grapple, trusting completely in the guidance of the Holy Spirit for success.

Many of the world's bishops were not enthusiastic about this council because they thought that it would simply end up restating everything that already had been clearly defined in Scholastic or Thomistic Catholic textbooks. Indeed, many members of the powerful Roman Curia wanted the council to do exactly that and to issue further warnings to the modern world, to Protestants and to liberal theologians about the error of their beliefs and way of life. When some of the initial drafts of the council documents appeared to be exactly that—restatements of Scholastic theology and warnings to the world—Pope John took a bold step. In an address to the entire council,

> *[H]e disassociated himself from the Curia's narrow defensive view of the council and urged the bishops instead to undertake a great renewal of updating of the Church. Unlike the prophets of doom and gloom among his counsellors, he said, he preferred to take an optimistic view of the course of modern history. And he emphasized the need for the bishops to take a pastoral approach: They must not engage in sterile academic controversies, but must find meaningful, positive, and fresh ways of stating the Church's age-old doctrine.[7]*

This is precisely what began to happen. The assembled bishops excitedly drew on their own experience and on the valid insights of the theologians who served as *periti*, expert advisors. The bishops formulated documents that were both faithful to the Catholic tradition and applicable to the needs of the time—stated in fresh, up-to-date language with many references to the Bible and to the fathers of the Church. Pope John's pictorial image of why he called the council, opening a window to let in some fresh air, was beginning to come to pass.

Still there were problems and struggles with what the council said and how it was put into effect; but Pope John XXIII's prayer for a "new Pentecost" was answered, as was remarkably demonstrated by a new wave of the Holy Spirit's working that was experienced by Catholics beginning only two years after the council's close. The Pentecostal movement or charismatic renewal in the Catholic Church was only one of a number of clear signs that a new age of the Holy Spirit's work to renew the Catholic Church had begun.

The world mourned in 1963 when Pope John XXIII died after the first session of the council. He had faithfully done the great work the Lord had given him to do as pope (for only four years and seven months), and the work of Vatican II was continued under the able leadership of Pope Paul VI.

the SECOND VATICAN COUNCIL
to POPE BENEDICT XVI

When the beloved Pope John XXIII died, the task of directing Vatican II fell into the hands of Pope Paul VI (1963–1978). Although this was certainly one of the most exciting and productive times in the history of the Catholic Church, it was also one of the stormiest for the successor to the chair of Saint Peter. Pope Paul VI was not only challenged to conduct the council and bring it, with God's help, to a successful conclusion, but he was also called to oversee the implementation of the council—bringing it from documents on paper into the reality of the life of the Catholic Church in the world.

In order to evaluate how successfully the teachings of the Vatican II have been carried out, it is essential to know precisely what the council taught. Although the decrees and constitutions of Vatican II are not presented as precise, infallible definitions, the Catholic Church believes that what is contained in those documents was guided by the Holy Spirit as a word for our age, giving direction for the future of the Catholic Church and the world. In his apostolic letter beginning the new millennium,

Pope John Paul II called the teachings of Vatican II a "sure compass" to guide the Church in this new era.[1] Pope Benedict XVI referred to this in his first papal homily.

The official teachings of the twenty-one ecumenical councils of the Catholic Church, including Vatican II, have obligatory force for Catholics. Hence Catholics should study carefully what this council teaches, as well as become familiar with the major teachings of the twenty other ecumenical councils of the past.

What follows is a brief summary of the teaching of most documents of the Second Vatican Council. These documents may be divided into two categories: those that concern the life of the Catholic Church itself, including its relationship with other Christians, and those that concern the Catholic Church's relationship to the world, including non-Christians. A fuller discussion of these documents and the impact of the Second Vatican Council may be found in my book *Vatican II: The Crisis and the Promise* (Servant, 2005).

DOCUMENTS ON THE LIFE
OF THE CATHOLIC CHURCH

(Including Its Relationship With Other Christians)

The Dogmatic Constitution on the Church (Lumen Gentium). The bishops of Vatican II wrote two dogmatic constitutions, which are authoritative summaries of the official teachings of the Catholic Church in areas of doctrine. These two constitutions deal with essential elements of the Catholic Church's understanding of itself.

We noted earlier that the sudden end of the First Vatican Council prevented that council from considering the roles and responsibilities of bishops, priests, religious or laypersons. The statement of the First Vatican Council about the pope's primacy and infallibility was, of course, very important (and was reaffirmed in *Lumen Gentium*), but it left Catholics with an incomplete picture of their Church. The Dogmatic Constitution on the Church of Vatican II completed what the First Vatican Council had begun. Even some of the chapter headings of this document indicate this: the People of God, Laity, Religious and so on. The basic content of each chapter, summarized, is:

1. *The Mystery of the Church:* This first chapter stresses that the Church is more than a human institution. The Church is a mystery in the same way Jesus Christ is a mystery: a union of the human and the divine. The Church is a sacrament, or a visible continuation in the world, of Jesus Christ, its founder.

2. *The People of God:* This new guiding image for the Church stresses that the Church is the *people* of the new covenant chosen by God to be his own, his body, in the world.

3. *The Church Is Hierarchical:* This chapter affirms that the Church Jesus founded is built upon recognized ordained leaders who are a gift to God's people to lead them in carrying on Jesus' mission in the world. The ministries of the pope, bishops, priests and deacons are discussed.

4. *The Laity:* This section addresses the sharing in the priesthood, kingship and prophetic role of Jesus Christ of those Catholics who are not ordained nor dedicated by vows to religious life. This chapter was a breakthrough in

recognizing the active role and full dignity of laypersons in the Catholic Church. They are *not* second-class citizens but full participants in the mission of Christ.

5. *The Call of the Whole Church to Holiness:* This chapter emphasizes that *all* Christians are called to holiness. All Christians, not just priests and religious, are called to be saints. It recognizes that each vocation possesses its own unique way to achieve holiness.

6. *Religious:* This chapter acknowledges the important leadership role in the Church of those whose lives are dedicated to Christ through the vows of poverty, chastity and obedience. It stresses the value and relevance of the religious life to the modern world based on these three evangelical counsels.

7. *The Pilgrim Church:* This chapter reminds us that the Church is only a pilgrim on the earth; its goal and true home is union with the Lord in heaven. The chapter also emphasizes the present union or communion of the pilgrim Church on earth with those members of the Church being purified in purgatory and with those who have already attained the glory of heaven. This fellowship is known as the communion of saints.

8. *Our Lady:* The final chapter of the document is devoted to the special role of Mary as mother and model of the Church and her role in God's plan of salvation. It is significant that rather than having a separate document on Mary, as some proposed, the council fathers included discussion of Mary in this document to emphasize that Mary is, first and foremost, a *member* of or part of the Church and not "above" the Church. Mary, too, is a

member of the community of believers saved through the grace of Jesus Christ.

Although this constitution is the central document of Vatican II, other decrees of the council expand what is contained in summary form in this constitution. They are the Decree on the Apostolate of Lay People *(Apostolicam Actuositatem)*; the Decree on the Ministry and Life of Priests *(Presbyterorum Ordinis)*; the Decree on the Training of Priests *(Optatam Totius)*; the Decree on the Appropriate Renewal of Religious Life *(Perfectae Caritatis)*; and the Decree on the Pastoral Office of Bishops *(Christus Dominus)*. All of these decrees are the further development and specification of the principles that are found in the related chapters of the Dogmatic Constitution on the Church. This does not imply that they are less important documents of Vatican II. To the contrary, these decrees were necessary to complete the full Catholic understanding of the different ways of life and vocations that join to make up the entire people of God. They are like parts of a puzzle which, when fitted together properly, form a beautiful picture—in this case the full membership of the Catholic Church.

Decree on Eastern Catholic Churches
(Orientalium Ecclesiarum).

The Catholic Church is not limited to the Roman rite. This decree proclaims the beauty and importance of the Eastern Catholic Churches, that is, churches that are subject to the governing authority of the pope but possess rites other than the Roman rite. Too often in the past, these churches were overlooked or not understood to be truly part of the Catholic Church because of their different traditions or smaller numbers.

This decree shows how the Eastern Catholic Churches demonstrate the diversity and universality of the Catholic Church and enhance its beauty. Unity does not mean uniformity for Catholics.

Constitution on the Sacred Liturgy (Sacrosanctum Concilium). This was the first document to be discussed and voted on by Vatican II and the document that had the most immediate effect on the actual daily life and experience of Catholics. The groundwork for this constitution had been laid by liturgical scholars who had been studying and discussing liturgical renewal since the late nineteenth century.

A key phrase of the constitution is "active participation." Laypeople are not to be spectators at the liturgy but are to be actively involved in worshiping God. Many of the practical changes advised by this constitution have as their goal to make it possible (or easier) for people to understand and participate in the liturgy. For example, Mass said in the vernacular, the language of the people, was presented as a possible practice and was quickly adopted by most bishops of the world in their dioceses.

If anything, the most frequent criticism of this document is that its directives were put into practice too quickly or without adequate explanation, making it difficult for many Catholics to adjust to it. In some places, problems were created when priests violated some of the clear directives of the constitution, such as that no one was to diverge from the authorized eucharistic prayers at Mass. Confusion was also caused when unauthorized ministers were allowed to perform certain rites. Such abuses caused unnecessary tension and confusion among Catholics.

The constitution also did an important service in clarifying what Catholics believed about the liturgy, such as explaining how Catholics understand the Mass as a perpetuation or re-presentation of the one eternal sacrifice of Christ on Calvary, not as re-sacrificing Christ. This constitution also broadened the use of sacred Scripture in Mass readings and homilies, restored the permanent diaconate and revived the Rite of Christian Initiation of Adults (RCIA).

Dogmatic Constitution on Divine Revelation (Dei Verbum). *Dei Verbum* continues the guidance and encouragement given to biblical scholars that began with Pope Pius XII's encyclical *Divino Afflante Spiritu*. This constitution encourages use of modern methods of biblical exegesis while reminding scholars that the final judgment on the validity of their findings rests with the pope and bishops, who comprise the Catholic Church's *magisterium*, or teaching office.

This constitution states that God reveals his truth through human beings, so the Bible may be considered "the words of God, expressed in human words."[2] The document summarizes how Catholics understand God's truth to have been transmit-ted or passed on in the Church. It explains that although there is only one source of revelation, God himself, his truth comes to the Church through the unified and interdependent chan-nels of sacred Scripture, sacred Tradition (authentic Christian teaching affirmed as true and transmitted within the Church over the course of many centuries) and the *magisterium* (or teaching office of the Church), which is a servant of God's word—listening to it, guarding it and teaching it faithfully.

After a review of the Old and New Testaments, the constitu-tion closes with a chapter on "Sacred Scripture in the Life of the Church," exhorting all Catholics, especially priests and religious, to study and read the Bible constantly, "[immersing] themselves in the Scriptures by constant sacred reading and diligent study."[3]

Declaration on Christian Education
(Gravissimum Educationis).

Education is a vital concern of Catholics and of all Christians. The need for true religious freedom for Christian schools, that they be given the same status and same opportunity for economic support as public schools, is acknowledged. Approaches to Christian education from a Catholic perspective are also examined.

The Decree on Ecumenism (Unitatis Redintegratio).

This document truly began a new era in the relationship of the Catholic Church with other Christians. Throwing off all triumphalism of the past, the Catholic Church openly acknowledged its share of the blame for the division of Christianity. The document states that Catholics are to regard other Christians as brothers and sisters in Christ even through they are separated by differences of belief and practice. The decree examines some of the differences separating Catholics from Protestants and from Orthodox Christians but emphasizes those beliefs that we hold in common.

In the chapter "Catholic Principles on Ecumenism," some practical guidelines are presented for how Catholics should engage in ecumenical activity, seeking unity with other Christians. Catholics are encouraged to take the initiative, to make the first approach to build unity with other Christians. The most significant warning for Catholics is to avoid a "false conciliatory approach"—a false ecumenism that ignores the real differences that divide Christians or that falsifies Catholic beliefs for the sake of unity.[4]

For example, this decree and the Dogmatic Constitution on the Church state that only the Catholic Church possesses the fullness of the means of grace and salvation brought to mankind by Jesus Christ. Catholics also do not believe in receiving Holy Communion with other Christians until full church unity is restored with them (though bishops may authorize exceptions to this). Although Catholics may not want to highlight these beliefs in ecumenical situations or discussions, neither can Catholics deny or compromise them.

The Decree on Ecumenism assumes that genuine unity is based on truth. This means that all Christians must continue to be faithful to what they truly believe, trusting in the grace of God and the guidance of the Holy Spirit to bring us together as he wills. Until full unity is achieved, the decree encourages Catholics to join with other Christians in service, in praying together and in sharing our Christian lives in other ways, all to promote the unity of God's people.

DOCUMENTS ON THE CATHOLIC CHURCH'S RELATIONSHIP TO THE WORLD

(Including Non-Christian Religions)

Pastoral Constitution on the Church in the Modern World
(Gaudium et Spes).

This was the only document the council called a "pastoral constitution." The term *constitution* indicates its great importance for the life of the Church; the word *pastoral* tells us that it is not primarily concerned with presenting doctrine (though its teaching is based on doctrine) but with giving Catholics practical guidance.

This constitution is at the heart of Pope John XXIII's desire for *aggiornamento*, bringing the Church up-to-date by putting it in touch with the conditions and needs of the modern world. This constitution is divided into two sections: (1) a general presentation of the Church's understanding of man's situation today and of the Church's relationship to modern man; and (2) an examination of some specific areas of special urgency in the life of mankind today.

The basic premise of the first section is the dignity of the human person, created by God in his own image. The Church is not separated from the world and its problems but is part of them and desires to work together with all men of good will to seek solutions. The document boldly proclaims the Catholic Church's belief that the ultimate solution to all human predicaments and problems, and the fulfillment of all human hopes, is to be found only in Jesus Christ. Jesus, God's only-begotten Son, entered fully into our human condition and emerged victorious over all evil, sin and death, giving man the hope of sharing the same victory.

The second section of the constitution discusses specific areas: the dignity of marriage and family life, the proper development of culture, mankind's economic and social life, the political community, the fostering of peace and the establishment of a community of nations.

This brief summary only provides a glimpse of the broad scope of this longest of the documents of the Second Vatican Council. Although the document attempts to be practical, its main goal is to provide *principles* to guide Catholics in how to relate to the modern world and how to approach certain areas of special concern.

The Declaration on Non-Christian Religions (Nostra Aetate).
The Second Vatican Council also took a positive look at non-Christian religions. This document states that the Catholic Church respects whatever is true and good in these religions and even indicates that God, in his mercy, can grant salvation to those who have not yet accepted Christianity but who follow the truth as it is known to them through their consciences. Yet the document also stresses that Christians must never cease to proclaim to non-Christians the full saving message of Jesus Christ, the only Savior of mankind. Many may be lost who do not hear that message.

A large proportion of the declaration concerns the Jewish people, who have a special relationship to Christians through Abraham, Moses, the prophets and all who faithfully prepared the way for the coming of Christ. All anti-Semitism or discrimination against the Jewish people is vigorously rejected by this document.

Decree on the Church's Missionary Activity
(Ad Gentes Divinitus).

Some Catholics have falsely concluded from reading the Declaration on Non-Christian Religions that there is no longer a need for missionary activity directed toward the evangelization and conversion of non-Christian people. This decree makes very clear what the Declaration on Non-Christians implies, that the command of Jesus to "make disciples of all nations" (Matthew 28:19) is absolutely true and necessary today. This decree calls for a vibrant missionary outreach aimed at converting to Jesus Christ all who have not heard or accepted the gospel. The decree also gives practical instruction about how the missionary endeavor of the Catholic Church is to be organized and effectively carried out today.

Declaration on Religious Liberty (Dignitatis Humanae). This is another landmark in Catholic thought. For centuries Catholics accepted the premise that freedom should only be granted to those whose beliefs were true; it was assumed that governments had a right to suppress false religions. This declaration proposes that all persons should have the liberty to hold and practice whatever religion they wish without coercion, as long as they respect the common good and the right of others to practice their beliefs. The basis of this document is a deepened awareness of the dignity of the human person, whose freedom of choice in religion God fully honors. All persecution and denial of human rights because of religious beliefs are clearly condemned by this declaration.

Decree on the Means of Social Communication (Inter Mirifica). This decree presents important principles and moral guidelines for the use of means of social communication, a subject that is very important in this age of exploding growth of the communications media and the use of propaganda to influence the mass society of the modern age. This declaration is only a beginning, for much more teaching of the Church is needed to guide Catholics and the world in this controversial area.

THE ACHIEVEMENTS OF VATICAN II

Vatican II renewed the life of the Catholic Church and put it in a more positive, open relationship with other Christians, non-Christians and the modern world.

The Catholic Church's Inner Life.

There were a number of important changes in the Catholic Church's inner life. Theology based on Saint Thomas Aquinas and the schools of the Middle Ages, though still respected by the Catholic Church, was no longer seen as the *only* legitimate Catholic approach to theology. New freedom was given to Catholic biblical exegetes, historians and other scholars to explore new approaches to their fields of study. The bishops at Vatican II attended lectures by noted contemporary theologians such as Karl Rahner, s.j., and Yves Congar, o.p., which influenced their theology and even their voting at council sessions.

Within the Catholic Church the role and authority of the bishops was given greater emphasis, and bishops were encouraged to work collegially, actively supporting and cooperating with each other and with the pope. The council called for a regular synod or gathering of bishops to advise the pope on important matters and for the establishment and recognition of episcopal conferences in the various nations or territories. Bishops were called to be true fathers and shepherds to God's people.

Religious men and women were encouraged to renew their orders, basing them more fully on the spirit of their founders and adapting their orders to the conditions of modern life. Priests too were given a fuller sense of their pastoral role and the need to work together and support each other in union with their bishop.

An almost revolutionary idea was the importance of the role of laypeople in the Catholic Church. Laypeople received a sense of their responsibilities in carrying on the mission of Christ and of the Church, with the guidance of the clergy and yet not dependent on them to take all the initiatives. The importance of married and family life, as well as the single vocation, was stressed many times in the council documents. Laypeople realized more fully that Christian holiness was not just for priests and religious but for them too.

The reform of the sacred liturgy made the Mass and other liturgical celebrations more meaningful and understandable to most Catholics. Participation in the liturgy, especially through music and shared responses, did increase visibly. Reading the Bible also became more important in the daily life and worship of Catholics, and many new aids to studying Scripture became available.

The Catholic Church's Relationships Outside of Itself.

In terms of the Catholic Church's relationship to other Christians, non-Christians and the world, many advances were made. *Ecumenism* was a new word to most Catholics, but soon a primary concern for Catholics was to learn to relate to other Christians as brothers and sisters in Christ and to value the true and positive elements in their traditions and churches. Ecumenical organizations, prayer groups and other associations were begun and have received much Catholic support.

Most Catholics did not feel the immediate impact of the council's teaching on non-Christian religions and missionary activity, but at least there grew an awareness among some Catholics that not all non-Christians were necessarily condemned to hell. A more positive attitude and relationship between Catholics and Jewish believers have developed in many places.

The greatest impact of the council with regard to the world has been the impetus for Catholics to get more involved in the affairs of society, especially to promote justice, peace and the defense of human life. This is based on a deeper understanding of the freedom and dignity of the human person. The quest for social justice, concern for the poor and seeking freedom from political, social and economic oppression of people has swept through the Catholic Church, as well as a vital "pro-life" movement.

Renewal Movements and Groups.

Although Vatican II did not call for the formation of movements or groups of renewal (except for encouraging Catholic Action in the Decree on the Apostolate of the Laity), the outpouring of the grace of God and the power of the Holy Spirit occasioned by the council led to many manifestations of renewal.

Both the Dogmatic Constitution on the Church and the Decree on the Apostolate of the Laity spoke of the importance of the working and gifts of the Holy Spirit. Only two years after the close of the council in 1965, a great wave of the power and gifts of the Holy Spirit began to sweep through the Catholic Church, known as the Pentecostal Movement or Catholic charismatic renewal. Hundreds of thousands of Catholics have been baptized in the Holy Spirit since then. Pope Paul VI gave his official approval to this renewal in 1975, and it later was confirmed by Pope John Paul II. Many Catholics believe that Pope John XXIII's prayer for "a new Pentecost" in the Catholic Church has been answered powerfully through this new outpouring of the Holy Spirit.

The list of renewal movements that have begun and groups that have formed since the close of the council is truly amazing: biblical renewal, renewal of married and family life, retreat movements and renewal of spiritual direction, renewal of preaching and new evangelization, renewal of basic Christian commitment (the RCIA) and the emergence of new forms of Christian community, parish renewal and movements concerned with social justice and protection of human life (the pro-life movement). Cardinal Joseph Ratzinger, former head of the Vatican's Sacred Congregation for the Doctrine of the Faith and now Pope Benedict XVI, was quoted in 1984 as saying:

> *What's hopeful at the level of the universal church—that is happening right in the heart of the crisis of the Church in the Western world—is the rise of new movements which nobody had planned and which nobody has called into being, but which have sprung spontaneously from the inner vitality of the faith itself. What is manifested in them is something like a pentecostal season in the church. I am thinking, say, of the charismatic movement, of the Cursillos, of the movement of the Focolare, of the neo-catechumenal communities, of "Communion and Liberation."* [5]

While acknowledging that these movements occasionally have problems (since there are always some problems where there is real life), Cardinal Ratzinger stressed that "the intense life of prayer," the "joy of faith" and "new vocations" springing from these movements make it evident that they are truly God's way of renewing the Catholic Church in our time. No human being planned or organized many of these movements; they were results of God's direct action and an expression of his love for his people.

PROBLEMS AND CHALLENGES EMERGING IN THE AFTERMATH OF THE COUNCIL

Catholics should praise and thank God for the achievements of Vatican II and for the movements of renewal that have sprung up in the Catholic Church since then. However, it is also true that some very difficult problems and crises have followed in the wake of the council. Some people have commented that when John XXIII "opened the window" of the Catholic Church to let in some "fresh air," some undesirable things blew in, besides the Holy Spirit. John XXIII warned against "prophets of gloom," but still we would be naive to ignore the serious difficulties that began to plague the Catholic Church after Vatican II.

It is important to understand from the beginning that some of the serious problems since the council have come from a misunderstanding or a false application of what the council actually taught. This is why it is necessary to study what the Vatican II documents actually say. Many Catholics began to believe or to do things that they thought were in the spirit of Vatican II but that violated what the council actually taught. Some Catholics said that these official teachings were just a starting point and so proceeded to experiment and pursue new ideas that had little or no basis in the council documents. The lesson that the Catholic Church has learned is that only what Vatican II actually taught was assuredly guided by the Holy Spirit and that Catholics need the guidance and wisdom of the *magisterium* or official teaching office of the Catholic Church to correctly carry out the council's teaching or to set off in new directions.

Also it is necessary to understand that many of the difficulties in the Catholic Church since Vatican II have nothing to do with the council but were problems created by the increasingly secular and godless culture of the world in which the Church lives. In fact, without Vatican II, the Catholic

Church would be in an even worse position to deal with these challenges from outside of itself.

Let us briefly summarize some of the problems that have arisen since 1965 that may be related to Vatican II or to a false understanding of the council. Many of these difficulties are connected with a misunderstanding of what the council taught about being open to or in touch with the modern world.

Thousands of priests and religious left their ministries or communities because their spiritual mission and ministry no longer made sense to them. They thought that Vatican II encouraged them to get involved with the world, to do the same things as secular social workers, psychologists or others serving the needs of people. Many priests and religious apparently did not understand all that Vatican II had to say about their spiritual identity and mission and their continued need to be guided by those in authority over them in the Church.

Some bishops, it appears, confused the council's exhortation to be more pastoral—being fathers and shepherds to God's people—with being permissive—allowing Catholics to do or think whatever they wanted. There was a new spirit of experimentation rampant in the Catholic Church, which some bishops did not know how to control properly.

In the area of liturgy, many Catholics lost the sense of the sacred in their worship. Participation was emphasized, but often the sense of reverence in the presence of God was sacrificed in the process. Many unauthorized experiments and innovations added to the difficulty of adjusting to proper changes that were already challenging enough, such as liturgy in the language of the people (vernacular) and with the priest facing the congregation. Related to this was a general loss of understanding the *Church as a mystery* of God's work and presence in the world. Some Catholics began to look at the Church as just another human organization.

With the encouragement of new approaches to biblical scholarship and other fields of study, some theologians and Catholics overlooked the role of the pope and bishops as the authentic teachers and guardians of the faith. Many Catholics were confused when the theories of new biblical scholars were presented in church on Sunday as absolute, dogmatic truth. Many Catholics began to accept the scholars' views as final and turn to them for guidance. When the *magisterium* tried to correct this, there sometimes developed a conflict between scholars and bishops or scholars and the pope; some Catholics began to value the opinions of the scholars more heavily than the Church's official teaching through the pope and bishops.

Related to this was a crisis in Christian education, particularly religious education. Children and young people were not taught the basics of the Catholic faith in some places because of the reaction of adults in the Church against dogma. Sometimes what was presented in religious education as Catholic truth was really the common opinion of the age, such as the denial of original sin. Method in religious education and clarification of values sometimes overshadowed the faithful teaching of Catholic doctrine in its fullness.

There was a considerable undermining of traditional Catholic moral teaching after Vatican II, because many Catholics interpreted being in touch with the world or open to the world to mean looking to the secular world for values and moral guidance. This opened the door to sexual permissiveness, the separation of sexuality from childbearing and motherhood and many other false values. The rise in divorce, artificial means of birth control and even abortion among Catholics—things that were rare among Catholics forty years ago—is evidence of the undermining of the Catholic way of life.

From the Declaration of Non-Christian Religions, some Catholics got the false impression that there was no need for converting non-Christians to Jesus Christ. Also, some Western Catholics felt encouraged to look to other religions for guidance and to adopt their forms of prayers, as if the Catholic faith and spiritual tradition was in some way inadequate or incomplete.

The Decree on Ecumenism was sometimes thought to teach that all Christian churches were the same (or at least equally true), and Catholics, even priests, began to ignore the official directives of the Catholic Church on intercommunion and other areas. Instead of explaining the Catholic faith to other Christians in its fullness, some Catholics began to water down or deny certain aspects of their faith in ecumenical dialogue. Sadly, some Catholics have even left the Catholic Church to join other denominations, which they met through ecumenical contact, seeing them as more vibrant or more authentically Christian than the Catholic Church.

Finally, confusion regarding the Catholic Church's teaching about the need to serve the poor and liberate them from social, economic and political oppression has led some Catholics to ally themselves with atheistic or Marxist movements or to adopt Marxist beliefs and strategies. The primary mission of the Church to lead people to Jesus Christ and to worship him either is subordinated to the goal of liberation in this world or is forgotten altogether.

The list of challenges facing the Catholic Church after Vatican II goes on, but this will suffice to give some idea of the magnitude of the task of helping Catholics to understand Vatican II correctly. In summary, Cardinal Ratzinger commented that instead of bringing a new unity to the Catholic Church, in some ways Vatican II has created greater dissension, especially in the West. Instead of seeing renewal sweep through the Church, we observe increasing decadence and confusion in many quarters.

It appears that the Catholic Church has undergone a time of purification. Jesus seems to be calling Catholics to a decision: either to follow him more closely by living in obedience to his teaching and to the authority he has established in the Church, or to follow the ways of the world, which are in rebellion against the teaching of Christ and the Church's leaders and their guidance. The four popes whom God has raised up since Vatican II began have had the burden and responsibility of leading the Catholic Church through this difficult but exciting time of change, renewal and purification.

POPE PAUL VI (1963–1978)

After long years of service to the Church, Giovanni Montini was named archbishop of Milan in 1954 and later was raised to the cardinalate by John XXIII. He was a recognized leader in the first session of Vatican II. As pope, Paul VI led the Catholic Church through one of the most crucial stages of its history. The monumental changes decreed by Vatican Council II led the Church out of the Tridentine period (in which the Catholic Church was guided primarily by the decrees of the Council of

Trent) to a new period. Pope Paul VI, however, realized the importance of maintaining continuity with the past, since this was not a new Catholic Church but just another step ahead in its long history and tradition. Therefore, Pope Paul VI wanted to implement the changes of Vatican II slowly and gradually. Many have criticized him for moving too slowly, but the wisdom of his approach is apparent even now.

Pope Paul VI's activity certainly was not all related to Vatican II. Like Saint Paul, he had a mission to the world. He addressed the United Nations and called for an end to war. He traveled to the Holy Land, where he greeted the Eastern Orthodox patriarch with the "kiss of peace" on the Mount of Olives. He traveled to Eucharistic Congresses in India, Colombia and Italy and visited sites of natural disaster (Pakistan) and sites sacred to the Virgin Mary (Fatima and Ephesus). He also met to seek unity with the leading bishop of the Anglican Church, Michael Ramsey. Pope Paul VI was truly an apostle of peace.

Pope Paul VI was also a powerful teacher. He spoke of the true nature of the Church in his first encyclical, *Ecclesiam Suam* (1964), and then followed in the tradition of the great Catholic social encyclicals with *Populorum Progressio*, "On the Development of Peoples," in 1967. He encouraged all Catholics to pray the rosary for peace in his fourth encyclical in 1966, and he explained the value of priestly celibacy in an encyclical the following year.

Pope Paul VI's teaching was wide-ranging, and it is ironic that he is only remembered by some Catholics for his encyclical *Humanae Vitae* (1968), which summoned married Catholics to regulate births only by natural means, reaffirming the Catholic Church's traditional teaching.

Pope Paul VI also raised the number of cardinals and made the college of cardinals more international in representation. He added the first women religious in history to work in the Roman Curia. He restored the office of permanent deacon to the status it had in the early Church. He recognized the new role of the bishops by calling a number of synods of bishops to advise him. Although his failing health limited his activity toward the end of his papacy, Pope Paul VI will be remembered as the key figure to maintain the balance after Vatican II between implementing changes in the Church and keeping the Church truly faithful to its traditions.

Many outstanding Catholics share in the history of this period: Dom Helder Camara, archbishop of Recife, Brazil, was known for his commitment to the poor; Dorothy Day, cofounder of the Catholic Worker Movement, was also widely admired, as was Mother Teresa of Calcutta, whose Missionaries of Charity now serve around the world. They represent thousands of other Catholics who worked heroically in this period to advance God's kingdom.

POPE JOHN PAUL II (1978–2005)

After the sudden death of Pope John Paul I after only thirty-three days as pope, the cardinals met again and elected the first non-Italian pope since 1522, Cardinal Karol Wojtyla, archbishop of Krakow, Poland. He was the first pope from a communist-dominated nation. His twenty-seven-year pontificate would be the third longest in history. The impact of his pontificate was so profound that many have dubbed him "John Paul the Great"— a title that only time can test.

From the beginning of his pontificate, John Paul II invited the world to reject fear and to "open wide the doors to Christ." This missionary pope proclaimed the gospel and strengthened the Church by traveling to every corner of the globe. It is estimated that his travels as pope were equivalent to three times the distance between the earth and the moon (over seven hundred thousand miles) and that no person in history has spoken to so many people—hundreds of millions—personally and through the media, in many cultural contexts. One papal innovation was his World Youth Days, where hundreds of thousands of young people imbibed Pope John Paul's exuberance and warmth and his message of hope and encouragement in Jesus Christ.

Pope John Paul II was equally potent in his teaching. He was a first-rate philosopher, as evidenced in his works *The Acting Person* and *Love and Responsibility*. He was able to translate profound concepts into practical pastoral teaching, as in his "theology of the body." A key to much of his thought was the inherent dignity of each human person, a concept that is at the heart of the pro-life movement and all Catholic social teaching.

As a young bishop Karol Wojtyla had participated in the Second Vatican Council, which deeply influenced his life and work. As pope he saw his primary task as the full and faithful implementation of the Second Vatican Council, which he called "the great grace bestowed on the Church in the twentieth century" and a "sure compass" to guide the Church as it entered the third millennium.[6] He authorized a universal catechism (first published in 1992) to present Catholic doctrine in light of the council. He called regular synods of bishops to discuss the implementation of the council in many areas, as well as addressing other pastoral concerns, and he wrote pastoral letters on important topics, like the dignity and vocation of women *(Mulieris Dignitatem)*.

Some of Pope John Paul's fourteen encyclical letters reflect concerns of the council, such as promoting social justice, ecumenism (Christian unity) and missionary activity. In some of these areas progress was made during his pontificate, as when the 1997 "Joint Declaration on Justification" was approved by both the World Lutheran Federation and the Catholic Church. Other encyclicals reflect the pope's own deep faith and spirituality, such as encyclicals on divine mercy *(Dives in Misericordia;* he also canonized the Polish "saint of divine mercy," Sister Faustina Kowalska), on Mary *(Redemptoris Mater;* his personal motto was *Totus Tuus,* "Totally yours, Mary") and on the Eucharist *(Ecclesia de Eucharistia)*.

John Paul II was a decisive leader who fearlessly lived and proclaimed a message of peace and reconciliation. Many informed observers attributed the downfall of Soviet domination in Eastern Europe in 1989, at least in part, to his moral influence and diplomacy. He first visited his homeland as pope in 1979, and he provided ongoing support for the nonviolent workers' movement in Poland led by Lech Walesa, who was awarded the Nobel Peace Prize.

John Paul II invited representatives of major world religions to Assisi in 1986 for a World Day of Prayer for Peace. He sought pardon for the sins of the Catholic Church, past and present, especially at the climax of his papacy—the "Great Jubilee" celebrating the two thousandth anniversary of the coming of Jesus Christ. John Paul II himself gave an example of forgiveness when he visited and forgave the young man, Mehmet Ali Agca, who attempted (almost successfully) to assassinate him in 1981.

The world of the twenty-first century is a difficult and perilous place. Pope John Paul II confronted confusion with truth, disunity with charity and fear with faith and hope. He called the Church to holiness through prayer, as exemplified by his friend (Blessed) Mother Teresa of Calcutta.

At John Paul II's death many challenges remained unresolved, such as accusations (many substantiated) of sexual abuse of minors by priests, especially in the United States. Worldwide the Church still faced the denial of rights and liberties in many countries and even militant and organized opposition. In other places, especially in the West, decline in the practice of the faith and confusion about its true meaning pointed to a need for renewal or a revitalization and clear direction of the renewal called for by the Second Vatican Council and the popes who sought to implement it. The time was certainly ripe for the "new evangelization"—a proclamation of the gospel of Jesus Christ to the world with renewed zeal—called for by John Paul II.

It would be the task of the man whom Pope John Paul II appointed to be prefect of the Sacred Congregation for the Doctrine of the Faith in 1981, Cardinal Joseph Ratzinger, to carry on this work of guiding the Catholic Church as the next successor of Saint Peter. He would do so with the courage and hope that characterized his close friend Karol Wojtyla, who in 2001 urged the Church to heed the call of Jesus to "cast into the deep" *(Duc in Altum!)*—into the vast ocean of the new millennium.[7]

POPE BENEDICT XVI (2005—)

As prefect of the Congregation of the Doctrine of the Faith for almost twenty-four years, the German-born Joseph Ratzinger was known to be a man for whom the truth (and its defense) was central. His service from the beginning of his priestly life was in the field of theology, and he served as theological advisor to Cardinal Josef Frings of Cologne at the Second Vatican Council. He was a cofounder of a "progressive" theological journal, *Concilium*, but when this journal began to diverge from what he thought was authentic Catholic teaching, he left and supported a new journal, *Communio*. He became known for his profound writings, especially his *Introduction to Christianity* (1968) and *Eschatology: Death and Eternal Life* (1977).

Although Joseph Ratzinger had spent his entire priestly life as a theologian, Pope Paul VI appointed him to the post of archbishop of Munich in 1977 and also named him a cardinal. As a pastor who gained a reputation as a fine theologian and an excellent listener and collaborator, he was a natural choice for Pope John Paul II to install as the prefect of the Vatican's doctrinal congregation, where he served with distinction. The nature of this office entails strong action to protect the faith, as Joseph Ratzinger did with regard to liberation theology in the 1980s and a number of investigations of the writings of theologians that appeared to compromise the Catholic faith. The portrayal of Joseph Ratzinger as simply a rigid doctrinal "watchdog" or "enforcer" is unfair, and the cardinals indicated their respect for him by electing him pope in 2005.

In choosing the name Benedict, Joseph Ratzinger indicated his desire to preserve and restore Western culture, as Saint Benedict did. The greatest challenge to the West, in his view, is the "dictatorship of relativism," which denies the existence of an objective moral order and objective truth.

In his first papal homily Pope Benedict expressed his commitment to carry out fully and faithfully the teaching of the Second Vatican Council, as Pope John Paul II had done so diligently. He said that his "primary commitment" was the restoration of Christian unity, that unity for which the Vicar of Christ must work tirelessly.[8]

If Pope Benedict seeks to teach and defend the truth, it is clear that he desires to do so in love and through patient dialogue, rather than through polemics and harsh condemnation. His first two encyclical letters (which surprised those who expected an "enforcer") were on love (specifically, that "God is love"—*Deus Caritas Est*) and on hope *(Spe Salvi)*. In his first papal visits, hope was his central message, focusing on the ultimate and sure hope that we find in Jesus and his gospel. Fear, of which the world is filled, must yield to the hope possessed by those who believe in God. In the United States he spoke of a "new Pentecost" and "a new springtime in the Spirit" for America, if Christians will pray and live in expectation of the outpouring of the Holy Spirit.[9]

Pope Benedict's interests are far-reaching. He has published more than fifty books in his career, and even as pope he published *Jesus of Nazareth*, which models how theologians are to present the Church's faith using sound Scripture scholarship.

Pope Benedict will likely continue his efforts to bring women into active roles in the Church and to promote a beautiful and solemn liturgy. When Pope John Paul II died just months before the World Youth Day scheduled for Cologne, Germany, Pope Benedict didn't miss a beat in attending this great event, held on the soil of his native land. Benedict continues to foster World Youth Days, such as in 2008 in

Australia. In this, as in many of his addresses, Pope Benedict stressed that Jesus Christ is the source of our hope: the hope of humanity and of each individual person. He also has voiced his support of new ecclesial movements, which he had said in 1985 were the "what is hopeful at the level of the universal Church … like a pentecostal season in the Church."[10] He held an international meeting of these ecclesial movements at Pentecost 2006, as Pope John Paul II had done at Pentecost 1998.

Pope Benedict's pontificate will not be without challenges. He inadvertently precipitated one challenge when, in an address at Regensburg University, he alluded to difficulties (from a Christian perspective) with certain Islamic beliefs and practices. Although initially Catholic-Islamic relations were tense in some quarters, in the end this opened up and promoted more honest dialogue, which is essential for authentic interreligious (and ecumenical) relations. Nonetheless, this event signaled the fact that relations between Christians and Muslims, as well as relations among other world religions, will be an area requiring much prayer and sensitivity in the twenty-first century.

The Church is irrevocably committed to her mission, given to her by Christ himself, to witness to the fullness of his gospel tirelessly and boldly, "in season and out of season" (2 Timothy 4:2). This "new evangelization," as Pope John Paul II termed it, includes the witness both to those who have not yet heard and believed the gospel of Christ (which includes about two-thirds of the world's population) and to those in traditionally Christian (including Catholic) countries who need to hear and embrace the gospel anew (to be "reevangelized").

Pope Benedict XVI, who celebrated his eighty-first birthday in 2008, has been a dynamic witness to the power of the gospel of Christ and of his truth in the world. He continues a line of exemplary popes of the nineteenth and twentieth centuries. Catholics can only thank the Lord for the blessing of these leaders, in whom Christ, the Good Shepherd, is seen (in faith) leading his Church forward until the time of the completion of his kingdom. Thanks be to God!

a PERSPECTIVE *on* CHURCH HISTORY *and on the* ROLE *of* MARY

There has been so much to learn in this brief history of the Catholic Church, and so much more could be said. There are many more great saints whose names have not even been mentioned who can inspire us and instruct us. There are many more crises and challenges whose lessons for God's people have not been explored.

What is most important, however, is not to remember all the facts and details but to gain the proper perspective on the history of the Catholic Church. Some may look at this history as simply human history, judging it according to the weaknesses and failings of the members of the Catholic Church, especially the popes and bishops, the Church's leaders. Catholic Christians look at the history of their Church from the perspective of faith, with the eyes of faith, so to speak. God has chosen a people to be his own, and he has made a sacred covenant with this people. He promised he would not break this covenant even if Christians were unfaithful at times.

This covenant is sealed by the blood of the only-begotten Son of God, Jesus Christ. Jesus promised to remain with his people until the end of time (see Matthew 28:20), and he has fulfilled his promise to send the Holy Spirit to guide God's people into the fullness of truth (John 16:12–15). The Church continues Jesus' mission and ministry in the world, sent out by him to "make disciples of all nations, baptizing them in the name of the Father and of the Son and of the Holy Spirit, teaching them to observe all that I have commanded you" (Matthew 28:19–20).

Knowing that his people would not be perfect or sinless, Jesus gave us a way of looking upon sin and dealing with it. This applies not only to individuals but also to all of God's people united as the body of Christ. He said, "Judge not, and you will not be judged; condemn not, and you will not be condemned" (Luke 6:37; see Matthew 7:1). We may recognize sin in other Christians or in the Church, but we are not authorized to sit in judgment. This judgment is reserved for the Lord (see John 5:22). Jesus even told the woman caught in adultery, "Woman,…has no one condemned you?" She said, "No one, Lord." And Jesus said, "Neither do I condemn you; go, and do not sin again" (John 8:10–11).

Jesus told his followers that they must forgive one another, and this too applies to the Church. Our Lord taught us to pray, "Forgive us our sins, for we ourselves forgive every one who is indebted to us" (Luke 11:4; see Matthew 6:12). Further, there is to be no limit to our forgiveness. Jesus told Peter not just to forgive seven times but "seventy times seven" (Matthew 18:22). When we look at the history of the Catholic Church, we see many occasions where God's forbearance and forgiveness have been needed. History also shows us that no matter how low the Church or individuals in the Church have fallen, God's grace has been there to forgive and to raise the Church up again. The history of the Catholic Church is a history of God's constantly forgiving and renewing his people.

This is the positive side of the history of the Church. God's grace has been stronger and more abundant than any human weakness or sin in the Church. As a matter of historical fact, no other human institution has existed for two thousand years, as the Catholic Church has.

The great English historian, [Thomas Babington] Macaulay, once described [the Church] in the eloquent words:

> *"There is not, and there never was on this earth, a work of human policy so well deserving of examination as the Roman Catholic Church. The history of that Church joins together the two great ages of human civilization. No other institution is left standing which carries the mind back to the times when the smoke of sacrifice rose from the Pantheon, and when camelopards and tigers bounded in the Flavian amphitheatre. The proudest royal houses are but of yesterday, when compared with the line of the Supreme Pontiffs. That line we trace back in an unbroken series, from the Pope who crowned Napoleon in the nineteenth century to the Pope who crowned Pepin in the eighth; and far beyond the time of Pepin does the august dynasty extend, till it is lost in the twilight of fable.*
>
> *"The republic of Venice came next in antiquity. But the republic of Venice was modern when compared with the Papacy; and the republic of Venice is gone and the Papacy remains. The Papacy remains, not in decay, not a*

mere antique, but full of life and youthful vigor. The Catholic Church is still sending forth...missionaries as zealous as those who landed in Kent with Augustine, and still confronting hostile kings with the same spirit with which she confronted Attila.... Nor do we see any sign which indicates that the term of her long dominion is approaching. She saw the commencement of all the governments and of all the ecclesiastical establishments that now exist in the world; and we feel no assurance that she is not destined to see the end of them all.

"She was great and respected before the Saxon had set foot on Britain, before the Frank had passed the Rhine, when Grecian eloquence still flourished in Antioch, when idols were still worshipped in the temple in Mecca. And she may still exist in undiminished vigor when some traveler from New Zealand shall, in the midst of a vast solitude, take his stand on a broken arch of London Bridge to sketch the ruins of St. Paul's."

That is the vision that amid the desolation of the present holds our gaze spell-bound. We observe the immortality, the vigorous life, the eternal youth of the old, original Church. And the question rises to many lips, and to the lips of the best among us: What is the source of this strong life? And can the Church impart it, and will she impart it, to the dying western world? [1]

When God gave us free will, he knew we would sometimes sin, even under the new covenant. Yet we also see in the history of the Catholic Church men and women who have used their free will to respond to God's grace and mercy. The saints of the Church and the admirable example of so many holy popes, consecrated women, martyrs, bishops and even children and young people who have given their lives to God inspire and show us the *true* nature of the Church—a holy nation, a people set apart or consecrated to God. As the Letter to the Hebrews says,

> *Therefore, since we are surrounded by so great a cloud of witnesses, let us also lay aside every weight, and sin which clings so closely, and let us run with perseverance the race that is set before us, looking to Jesus the pioneer and perfecter of our faith, who for the joy that was set before him endured the cross, despising the shame, and is seated at the right hand of the throne of God. (Hebrews 12:1–2)*

Let us look to the witnesses of the faith that we find so abundantly in the history of the Catholic Church and to Jesus himself, to find the courage to give our own lives fully to God and to his Church.

THE HOLY SPIRIT'S ONGOING WORK OF RENEWAL

Catholics understand that the Church is always being reformed or renewed. This is an important and continual work of the Holy Spirit. The Spirit is the life-principle of God's people, given to us by Jesus and the Father both to guide the Church and to constantly revitalize or renew it. The Holy Spirit is at work in the body of Christ to conform it and its members more fully to its head, Jesus Christ.

As we look at the history of the Catholic Church, it may appear that its life has gone in cycles or stages. At one stage the

Church is evidently strong and full of spiritual life and vitality. Then the Church seems to go into a period of decline, when crises besiege the Church or the spiritual vitality of God's people weakens or falls to a low level. At these low points it is easy to think that the Lord has abandoned the Church, just as this seemed to happen to the Jewish people at many points in the history of the old covenant. But it is often just when the Catholic Church seems to be in its worst condition that the Holy Spirit begins his work of renewal and revitalization.

The Holy Spirit is always available to bring new life to God's people. Sometimes the only reason that we don't see the Holy Spirit at work more powerfully in the Church is that we don't ask him. Jesus said that if a human father readily gives his sons and daughters good things, "how much more will the heavenly Father give the Holy Spirit to those who ask him!" (Luke 11:13).

The life of the Catholic Church is somewhat like our individual lives. It has its ups and downs. Periods of spiritual fervor and experience of God's presence are eventually followed by falling back into sin or feeling that God is absent or has abandoned us. The truth is that God is always there, for us and for the whole Church. As the book of Lamentations says so beautifully:

> *The steadfast love of the LORD never ceases,*
> *his mercies never come to an end;*
> *they are new every morning;*
> *great is thy faithfulness. (Lamentations 3:22–23)*

What are some of these advances and declines, the ups and downs, in the life of the Catholic Church? Catholic historian

Christopher Dawson has noted that the Catholic Church (particularly in the West) has experienced six ages, with each age beginning with a time of growth and the Holy Spirit's work of renewal, leading to a climax or height of Catholic life and culture and ending with a time of decline in the spiritual life and vibrancy of the Church or with another type of crisis.[2] According to Dawson:

The First Age of the Church began with the outpouring of the Holy Spirit at Pentecost, leading to the conversion of a significant proportion of the Roman Empire to Christianity, despite government persecution. This period ended not with spiritual decline but with the severe, empire-wide persecutions of the Catholic Church in AD 250 and at the beginning of the fourth century, in which many Christians lost their lives for their faith.

The Second Age of the Church began with the victory of Constantine, granting religious freedom to Christians in AD 313 and leading to the conversion of a large proportion of the Roman Empire to Christianity through the Holy Spirit's power. This was also the great age of spiritual and theological writings known as the Age of the fathers of the Church. The period ended with the political takeover of the Roman Empire by non-Christian tribes, culminating in the Islamic conquest of Jerusalem in AD 643.

The Third Age of the Church began with the conversion of certain tribes to Christianity (for example, the Franks) and was sparked by the Holy Spirit's renewal of the Church and missionary outreach begun by Pope Gregory I. This was the beginning of Christendom in the West, the time of the alliance between the Catholic Church and the political state, which reached its first climax during the reign of the emperor Charles the Great, "the New Constantine" (crowned AD 800). After his death the new Holy Roman Empire was divided, and the Catholic Church experienced a severe spiritual decline.

The Fourth Age of the Church began with the Holy Spirit's renewal of monastic life, which started at Cluny in AD 910 and reached even to the center of the Church with the reforms of Pope Gregory VII (who had been a monk of Cluny) in 1073. The spirituality, thought and culture of the Church reached its climax in this period in the thirteenth century through the mendicant orders of Saint Francis and Saint Dominic and the great Catholic schools and universities. But the most severe period of spiritual and intellectual decline in the Church's history began at the end of the thirteenth century, reaching its lowest point around 1500 with the Protestant Reformation.

The Fifth Age of the Church began with the Holy Spirit's renewal of Catholic life out of the turmoil of the Protestant Reformation in the sixteenth century. This great renewal reached its height at the end of the sixteenth century and in the early seventeenth century. After that the effects of the Enlightenment and the wars of religion began to seriously erode Catholic life, thought and spiritual strength, which reached a low point in the eighteenth century.

The Sixth Age of the Church began with the Holy Spirit's raising up strong popes and other Catholics in the nineteenth century who could respond to the attacks and influences of the

Enlightenment and to the political and ideological challenges facing the Church. Some have commented that every pope of the Catholic Church since the middle of the nineteenth century to the present has been a holy, strong and gifted leader in his own right. We must thank the Lord for this great gift. Since this is the age in which we live, it is difficult to determine whether we are in a time of advance or decline, but we must fervently seek God in prayer that the Holy Spirit would continue to guide, strengthen and renew the Catholic Church.

Based on this view of the six ages of the Church and its stages of advance and decline, a rough graph of the history of the Catholic Church might look something like this:

VISUALIZATION OF ADVANCE AND DECLINE IN THE CATHOLIC CHURCH'S HISTORY

Based on Christopher Dawson's *The Historic Reality of Christian Culture* (New York: Harper, 1960).

(Dawson's six ages are indicated by dotted lines.)

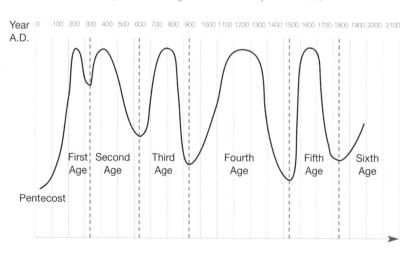

It is necessary to conclude this section with the caution that the history of the Church is very complex, and the division of it into ages or periods of advance or decline is simply a way of grasping some aspects of the truths of history. It is important to remember two things:

1. God is *always* with the Church, and the Holy Spirit is *always* at work, even in times of spiritual crisis or decadence among God's people.

2. Even in ages of strength in the Church in some area, there may be serious problems in other areas. An example of this is the fourth century, which produced great fathers of the Church such as Saint Athanasius, Saint Basil, Saint Gregory of Nyssa, Saint Gregory of Nazianzen, Saint Jerome and Saint Augustine but is also the century in which the Arian heresy almost split the Church in two, nearly leading a significant portion of the Church into false belief. Likewise, ages of decline in the general life of the Church often produced some of the greatest saints, such as Saint Catherine of Siena and Saint Bridget of Sweden during the Avignon papacy.

MARY AND THE CATHOLIC CHURCH

We will close this study of the history and meaning of the Catholic Church by considering the relationship of Mary, the Mother of God, to the Church's life and history. Mary is the most distinguished member of the Church, the first to hear the announcement of the birth of Israel's Savior and the first to wholeheartedly embrace and believe in that message.

Mary has long been recognized as a model or type of the Church. In her own person she summarizes what the whole Church is and is called to be—a disciple of Jesus Christ. Mary first heard the word of Jesus coming through the angel Gabriel at the Annunciation, and she believed in it. She not only bore the Son of God in her womb and raised him with Saint Joseph in his Jewish heritage but she also became a faithful follower of her Son right up to his death on Calvary, when she stood at the foot of the cross. With the other disciples Mary waited in prayer and faith for the sending of the Holy Spirit, and she was present as the Holy Spirit overshadowed those disciples when the Church was born at Pentecost, just as the Spirit of God first overshadowed her at the time of her Son's birth.

Mary is a model of the Church because she heard the word of God and did it (see Mark 3:35). This is the basic task of the Church and what discipleship is all about.

Some people object to focusing on Mary as a model of the Church because the Bible says little about her compared with Peter or Paul. But Mary's life is actually more like the life of most of the Church—quietly but faithfully doing God's will each day without receiving much attention for it. Mary lived her life pondering God's word in her heart (see Luke 2:51) and living it out in the simple way that God granted her to do it. She who was the most humble and obedient of Jesus' followers on earth has become the most highly exalted by God in heaven. Jesus himself said, "He who is least among you all is the one who is great" (Luke 9:48), and, "Whoever humbles himself will be exalted" (Matthew 23:12). Mary echoed this in her prayer, the Magnificat: "He [God] has regarded the low estate of his handmaiden.... Henceforth all generations will call me blessed; for he who is mighty has done great things for me, and holy is his name" (Luke 1:48–49).

Like Mary, the Church is called to be the faithful and obedient servant of God. Whatever good exists in the Church we attribute not to our own merits but to God, for "he who is mighty has done great things for [us], and holy is his name." The Church is to model itself upon Mary's faithful following of her Son, Jesus Christ.

MARY AS MOTHER OF THE CHURCH

Not only is Mary the model of the Church, but she is also its mother. From the cross Jesus told the beloved disciple, who represents the whole Church, "Behold, your mother!" (John 19:27). From the earliest times of the Church's history, Christians have looked upon Mary as their mother as well as the mother of Jesus. We, the Church, are the body of Christ. Just as Mary was the mother of Christ himself, she is now the spiritual mother of the body of Christ on earth, the Church.

As Vatican II's Dogmatic Constitution on the Church states so well, Mary continues to care for the Church on earth with "maternal charity" or motherly love. She prays for us and "by her manifold intercession continues to bring us the gifts of eternal salvation."[3]

Imagine Mary watching over the Church over the centuries, in the most fruitful times and the most difficult, continually praying for the strengthening and redemption of God's people. The Church is God's family, and we should thank God our Father for giving the Church a mother to intercede for us before his throne. She unites her prayers, as we all do, with the perfect intercession of the "one mediator between God and men, the man Christ Jesus, who gave himself as a ransom for all" (1 Timothy 2:5–6).

It is important for Catholics to enter into the faith of the Catholic Church concerning Mary's role in God's plan of salvation. This faith of God's people is vividly expressed over the centuries in Christian art, music and literature. The faith of the Catholic Church in Mary's role as intercessor and mother did not result from a doctrinal definition but from the experience of the Christian people having their prayers answered through Mary's intercession and through the Holy Spirit speaking to their hearts about Mary and her unique role in God's plan of salvation.

It should be mentioned that the *magisterium*, or authoritative teachers of the Catholic Church, have also had to caution Catholics occasionally about an overemphasis on Mary or an exaggeration of her status. Some Catholics have mistakenly approached Mary as if she were on the same level as Jesus Christ, which is to make her equal to God. Mary herself certainly gives us no reason to do this, for the whole goal of her life was to exalt God and to point to her Son, Jesus Christ. A true understanding of Mary will always recognize her subordination to God, receiving whatever role she has in God's plan from him. The final chapter of the Dogmatic Constitution on the Church of Vatican II and the Apostolic Exhortation of Pope Paul VI on the right ordering and development of devotion to the Blessed Virgin Mary (*Marialis Cultus*, February 2, 1974) both provide clear and complete explanations of how Catholics are to view Mary, the Mother of God.

APPEARANCES OF MARY
AND THEIR MESSAGE FOR TODAY

Throughout the Old Testament God brought special messages to his people of the old covenant by means of angels, a word that means "messenger." Isn't it appropriate that when God wishes to speak a special word to his people of the new covenant, he often sends the Mother of the Church, Mary, to be his messenger? This is part of Mary's role as the Church's mother—to announce the Lord's love and care for his people and to guide or warn God's children, her children, in times of special urgency.

Catholics are not required to believe as a doctrine of faith that Mary has appeared to people and spoken a word from God. The messages of the apparitions of Mary are called private revelations, which must be judged and evaluated by the public revelation given by God to his whole Church, especially through the Bible. However, certain appearances or apparitions of Mary have been widely accepted by Catholics and have been confirmed as authentic by popes, who have frequently visited the places of her appearances. We do not have time or space to speak of all the appearances of Mary, but some of the most significant will be mentioned here.

Our Lady of Guadalupe, 1531.
Only forty years after Christopher Columbus came to America, Mary appeared to a poor Aztec peasant, Juan Diego (now Saint Juan Diego, canonized by Pope John Paul II on July 31, 2002), in the Spanish colony of Mexico just outside Mexico City. The Spanish had destroyed all the pagan idols of

the Indians, but the harshness and misrule of the Spaniards made many Aztecs refuse to accept Christianity. Mary spoke a simple message of God's love and of her love for the Aztec people and asked that a church be built on the site. She instructed Juan Diego to tell the Spanish bishop, Zumarraga, all that he had seen and heard that day.

Zumarraga welcomed Juan Diego but asked him for some sign to confirm that Mary had truly appeared to him. Three days later, on December 12, the Virgin Mary told Juan Diego to cut some roses from a hilltop to bring to the bishop as a sign. Amazed to find Castilian (Spanish) roses growing in Mexico in December, Juan Diego cut them, and Mary arranged them in the fold of his mantle. When Juan Diego delivered them to the bishop, he was astonished to see imprinted on the mantle a beautiful image of a young woman with hands folded in prayer, surrounded by sunlight and standing on a dark crescent. The bishop believed and ordered a simple chapel be built by Christmas Day, when the first Mass was celebrated there.

The impact on the native people of this appearance of Mary was astounding. In their picture language the image represented a woman crushing the symbol of their serpent god, blotting out the image of their sun-god and worshiping the true God, whose sign (a black cross) was hung on a small golden brooch around her neck. Using these images, Juan Diego told his people that Mary's Son had died on the cross to free them from the bondage of false gods and make them children of a loving Father, to whom she was praying. The image portrays Mary as a merciful mother praying for her people. As the people brought their sick and needy to Mary to pray for them, miraculous healings and miracles began to occur.

The result of this one appearance of Mary was that during the next seven years (1532–1538), eight million native Mexicans were converted to the Lord and baptized—more than three thousand converts a day for seven years! Juan Diego stayed at the church for seventeen years, until his death, explaining what happened to him and the meaning of the image. Mary told Juan Diego, "I am your merciful mother, the merciful mother of all who live united in this land."[4] The people of both North and South America, with Mexico standing at the center, have taken this message as their own. One appearance of Mary has helped shape the history of two continents.

The Immaculate Conception, 1858, Lourdes.
There have been more appearances of Mary reported in the last 150 years than at any other time in the Catholic Church's history. It seems that God has some important things to speak to the Church in our day.

What is significant about Mary's appearance to a fourteen-year-old girl, Bernadette Soubirous, near Lourdes, France, is that Mary revealed to Bernadette a title that had been confirmed by an infallible statement of Pope Pius IX four years earlier. Mary told Bernadette, "I am the Immaculate Conception."[5] Young Bernadette repeated these words to a trusted friend without even understanding what they meant, not knowing that they referred to the special privilege granted by God to Mary to be conceived without original sin, given in view of her future role of bearing God's Son in her womb.

A spring of water that miraculously appeared at the site of Mary's appearances to Bernadette has been a source of thousands of medically verified healings that have occurred at

Lourdes and elsewhere that this water has been taken. This is another sign of Mary's motherly care and of her power to intercede on behalf of God's people.

Our Lady of Fatima, 1917.

We have already reviewed in a previous chapter the meaning of Mary's appearances to three children at Fatima, Portugal, in 1917. This message was summarized very well by Father Gerald Farrell, M.M., and Father George W. Kosicki, C.S.B., in their book *The Spirit and the Bride Say "Come!"*

In the apparition of July 13, 1917, Mary revealed that her Son wished to establish in the world devotion to her Immaculate Heart and that if this wish was complied with, Russia would be converted and there would be peace in the world. If not, she said, a second world war would break out during the pontificate of Pius XI, and Russia would spread her errors throughout the world, causing wars and persecutions of the Church. Later, in an apparition to one of the children, Lucy, on June 13, 1929, Our Lady made the request concerning the consecration of Russia more explicit, saying, "God asks the Holy Father, in union with all the bishops of the world, to make the consecration of Russia to my Immaculate Heart, promising to save it by this means."[6]

The promise made by Our Lady at the end of the July 1917 apparition still holds true: "But in the end my Immaculate Heart will triumph. The Holy Father will consecrate Russia to me, and it will be converted and some time of peace will be granted to humanity."[7]

We must understand that the most important point of the appearances of Mary is not predictions of the future. The basic message of Our Lady at Fatima is the urgent need of prayer, penance, fasting and conversion of heart to bring peace to the world and to lead all nations, and Russia in particular, to faith in Jesus Christ. She does add to this basic gospel message one other truth that Catholic Christians already know: Mary, through her loving, Immaculate Heart, is a powerful intercessor whom God has appointed to pray for the conversion of the nations to her Son. In praying the rosary, in particular, Catholic Christians draw closer to Christ and call on Mary to pray for us for the conversion of all peoples.

Cardinal Joseph Ratzinger, in discussing the message of Fatima in 1984, said:

> A stern warning has been launched from that place that is directed against the prevailing frivolity, a summons to seriousness of life, of history, to the perils which threaten humanity. It is that which Jesus himself recalls very frequently, "...Unless you repent you will all likewise perish" (Lk 13:3). Conversion—and Fatima fully recalls it to mind—is a constant demand of Christian life.
>
> ... [The messages of Fatima] only reconfirmed the urgency of penance, conversion, forgiveness, fasting.[8]

Mary's appearances are another sign of God's presence with his people, the Church. The belief that God has sent our mother, Mary, to speak his truth to us and to give us particular guidance for today should convince us that God is truly watching over and caring for us, his people.

It is worthy of note that the appearances of Mary are always made to God's "little ones" (the *anawim*), either to the young or the poor. Jesus himself said that unless we become as little children, we will not enter the kingdom of God (see Matthew 18:3). We must be simple in our faith, ready to hear God's word and respond to it, if we are to enter God's kingdom. Mary's appearances all illustrate and support this gospel truth.

In whatever way God speaks to us by the Holy Spirit, our responsibility is to listen to God and his messengers and to act according to his words. The Church will only be renewed and fulfill God's plan in our time—now—if we hear God speaking and respond to his word. Let us ask Mary to intercede for us as our mother and the Holy Spirit to guide and inspire us as we seek to follow Jesus Christ and do the will of our Father in heaven.

CHAPTER ONE

The Catholic Understanding of the Church

God's purpose in human history is to save mankind from sin and to offer it the gift of eternal life. He carries out this purpose by forming a people to be his own.

1. The Old Testament tells the story of God's calling forth and forming the people of the old covenant—the Hebrew or Jewish people.
2. The New Testament tells the story of God's calling forth and forming his new covenant people, through the work of the Son of God made man, Jesus Christ.

The name most often used for God's people of the new covenant is the "Church." Jesus himself speaks of forming his Church (see Matthew 16:18), which Saint Paul calls the "body" of Christ (Ephesians 5:23) and the bride of Christ (Ephesians 5:25–32; also see Revelation 19). In spite of the sins of the Church's members, Jesus Christ loves his Church and promised to remain with it (Matthew 28:20).

The Church is one. This is the first of the four marks or characteristics of the Church professed in the Nicene Creed: there is *one* Church, and the early Christians went to great lengths to preserve the Church's unity.

The Church is catholic. The one Church that Jesus founded is "catholic," meaning "universal" or embracing all peoples, races, nations and cultures. The Catholic Church received *Catholic* as part of its formal name because it was the only all-embracing, universal Church in the early centuries of Christianity.

The Church is holy. *Holy* means "set apart" or "consecrated" by God for himself and his purpose. Saint Peter calls the Church "a holy nation" (1 Peter 2:9). *Holy* does not mean "perfect" or "sinless," for Christ came to call not the perfect but sinners to repentance.

The Church is apostolic. The Church is "built upon the foundation of the apostles and prophets" (Ephesians 2:20), and through the bishops, the successors of the apostles, it carries on the mission of the first apostles to spread the gospel of Jesus Christ to the ends of the earth.

In spite of all that can be said about the Church, it remains a mystery of God's grace. God is mysteriously at work in human history to form this people and to protect and guide it, despite the weaknesses and sins of its members. The story of the Church is truly *our* story, as Catholic Christians.

CHAPTER TWO

The Church of the Apostles and the Fathers (AD 50–600)

The first century AD (AD 33–100) was a time of initial growth of Christianity, especially among the lower classes, due to heroic missionary efforts. The gospel was proclaimed by word of mouth and preaching. Christianity remained a small offshoot of Judaism, persecuted by the Roman emperors Nero and Domitian, who stirred suspicions about he Christian way of life and accused Christians of atheism for refusal to worship the emperor and Roman gods.

In the second century (AD 100–200) Christianity grew in numbers and influence despite sporadic persecution. Bishops Ignatius of Antioch, Polycarp and others were apostolic fathers who taught Christian truth and often witnessed to it with their lives (martyrs). Later, learned men (the apologists) defended the faith through philosophy and reason. The bishops of the Church confronted distortions of Christian teaching (the Gnostics, Marcion and others) and began to consider which Christian writings were God's Word for the whole Church (formation of the canon of Scripture).

By the third century (AD 200–300) schools of Christian teaching (catechetical schools) had arisen in major cities, producing such great teachers as Saint Clement and Origen of Alexandria, Egypt. Christianity was expanding, organizing and developing theologically until the persecution of Decius (AD 250) shook the Church and raised the question of how to deal with those who denied the faith (the sin of apostasy). Saint Cyprian of Carthage agreed with the pope (the bishop of Rome) that all who did penance could be readmitted. The Church was not just for the perfect but also for repentant sinners.

The fierce persecution of Diocletian (AD 303–311) was ended by the first Christian Roman emperor, Constantine. Constantine legalized Christianity for the first time and even passed laws favoring Christians. He also intervened in Church affairs by calling the first ecumenical (worldwide) council of Catholic bishops, the Council of Nicaea in AD 325, which attempted to stop Arius's denial of Christ's divinity. This heresy persisted, even supported by some bishops and emperors, until the Council of Constantinople in AD 381. There the efforts of pro-Nicenes Saint Athanasius of Alexandria, Saint Basil and the two Gregories (of Nazianzen and Nyssa) finally resulted in Arianism's defeat.

This century also marked the birth of the monastic or ascetic movement (Saint Antony of Egypt and Saint Pachomius, founders) and the emergence of great scholar-saints such as Ambrose, Jerome, John Chrysostom and Augustine of Hippo. Christianity became the established religion of the Roman Empire, and most people within the Empire became Catholic Christians, at least in name.

The Roman Empire was increasingly divided in the fifth century between the Greek-speaking East and the Latin-speaking West, which was eventually taken over by barbarian tribes. The popes, such as Leo I (the Great), had to protect God's people both spiritually and physically (from barbarian invaders). The heresy of Pelagius, denying the full effect of original sin, raged in the West, while in the East bishops and theologians struggled with clarifying how Christ's divine and human natures are joined. The Council of Chalcedon (AD 451) clarified this with Pope Leo I's help, but the Monophysites (who claimed Jesus was only divine) rejected Chalcedon's decision. Mary was proclaimed "Mother of God" *(Theotokos)* by the Council of Ephesus in AD 431.

The sixth century marks the end of the age of the fathers of the Church—the era of the great theologians of the first Christian centuries. East and West were preoccupied with survival in a new political order and with converting the barbarian conquerors of the Roman Empire. The monastic order of

Saint Benedict, founded in AD 529, became a great source of missionary outreach and of the preservation of Christian culture. The gospel was planted in Ireland by Saint Patrick and in Scotland by Celtic (Irish) monks.

CHAPTER THREE

The Church of the Middle Ages (AD 600–1300)

The seventh century (AD 600–700) began with the outstanding missionary work launched by Pope Gregory I (the Great), which led to the conversion of England by Saint Augustine of Canterbury and the Benedictine monks. The Third Council of Constantinople (AD 680–681) condemned Monotheletism, the belief that Jesus only had one divine will. The forces of Islam began to take over the Eastern (Byzantine) Empire.

In the eighth century the Benedictine missionary Saint Boniface led the conversion of Germany and helped forge an alliance between the pope and the king of the Franks, Pepin. This was the birth of Christendom, the close alliance of Church and state in the West, which lasted throughout the Middle Ages. Pepin's son, Charles the Great (Charlemagne), became king in AD 768 and was crowned Holy Roman Emperor by the pope in AD 800. Charles was a new Constantine who established the Catholic Church throughout his vast domain but also usurped authority from the pope and alienated the Byzantine Church and emperor by inserting the *filioque* clause ("and the Son") into the Nicene Creed. In the East the Second Council of Constantinople (AD 787) approved the veneration of icons or holy images.

The breakdown of Charles's empire led to the decline of the Church in the West during the ninth century, and increasing Islamic influence had the same effect on the Church in the East. The pope and the patriarch of Constantinople, Photius, broke off relationships between Christians of the East and West from 858 to 887. The fervor of monastic life and the life of the Church in general waned during this period, often called the Dark Ages. Saints Cyril and Methodius evangelized the Slavic peoples.

The founding of the monastery of Cluny in AD 910 began a renewal of the Church in the West in the tenth century. Other new monastic orders, such as the Camaldolese (Saint Romuald) and the Carthusians (Saint Bruno), added to the new fire of holiness. Otto I, the new Holy Roman Emperor from Germany, began to reform the Church in the West by appointing worthy popes and bishops. The controversy over this practice of lay investiture caused tension between popes and emperors throughout the Middle Ages.

Otto's practice of appointing strong popes finally led to the emergence of a great reforming pope from the Cluniac order, Pope Gregory VII. Gregory strove to end corruption in the Catholic Church and to free the Church from any control by emperors or secular rulers. He asserted the spiritual authority of the pope over any worldly ruler and even had the Holy Roman Emperor, Henry IV, approach him on his knees to beg forgiveness for rebelling against the Church. This century also marked the beginning of the tragic schism between the Eastern and Western Christian Churches in 1054, which has lasted even to the present. Pope Urban II launched the First Crusade in 1095 to free the Holy Land from Muslim control.

In the twelfth century the popes continued their active struggle to guide the Church and free it from the control of secular rulers. They continued the Crusades in the East, with only mixed results, and crusaded against new heresies in Europe, such as the Cathars (the "pure ones"). The Cistercian order gave rise to great saints, most notably Bernard of Clairvaux, but the monastic orders failed to solve the problems of heresy and increasing affluence and corruption in the Church. The founding of universities led to a new approach to theology—Scholastic theology—which employed philosophy and reason to illuminate the truths of faith. Saint Anselm of Canterbury and Peter Lombard were pioneers in this area. Soaring Gothic churches reflected new approaches to worship and prayer.

The thirteenth century was the height of the Catholic Church in the Middle Ages. The thirteenth-century popes, beginning with Innocent III, exercised full authority in both the spiritual and temporal sphere, as they continued to launch Crusades abroad (which largely failed) and established the Inquisition to root out heresy. They also called important reform councils: the Fourth Lateran in 1215 and the First and Second Councils of Lyons in 1245 and 1274.

But the greatest source of renewal of the Catholic Church came through the rise of the mendicant orders, which focused on living the poverty and humility of Christ. Saint Francis of Assisi, Saint Clare and Saint Dominic founded orders that bear their names. These new orders were the source of such great theologians as (the Franciscan) Saint Bonaventure and (Dominicans) Saint Albert the Great and Saint Thomas Aquinas. Dante's *Divine Comedy* was the greatest work of a

Christian literary revival, which also marked this century as the climax of Christian culture and civilization to date.

CHAPTER FOUR

The Late Middle Ages, Reformation and Counter-Reformation (AD 1300–1650)

The years 1300–1500, the Late Middle Ages, were a period of difficulty for the Roman Catholic Church. The popes resided in Avignon, France, for seventy years (1305–1376) to escape political pressures in Italy, but the prophetic voices of Saint Bridget of Sweden and Saint Catherine of Siena urged reform and called the popes back to Rome. A worse tragedy followed, however: the Great Schism of 1378–1417 in which two and later three men claimed to be the legitimate pope. The influence of the papacy was severely damaged. Englishman John Wycliffe and Czech John Hus further challenged the Church's teaching authority.

In spite of this there were signs of spiritual awakening. Catholic mysticism flourished in Holland, Germany and England. The modern devotion movement gave birth to *The Imitation of Christ* and other spiritual classics. Saint Joan of Arc's visions brought victory to France, and in the East the prayer of the heart *(hesychasm)* ushered in new spiritual life.

However, there were many underlying and immediate causes of the Protestant Reformation at the dawn of the sixteenth century. The financial difficulties of the popes led them to gain revenues for the Church by selling high offices to the wealthy or secular rulers, who had little concern for God's people. Other clergy were often uneducated and unfaithful to their vows of celibacy. Simony—the selling of spiritual goods and Church offices for money—was rampant.

The popes wished to raise money to keep the Church in the forefront of the Renaissance, the revival of learning and culture, but this and political involvements distracted them from the alarming spiritual sickness of the Church. Although Pope Julius II called the Fifth Lateran Council in 1512, few of its many reform decrees were implemented. Secular rulers (who were often bishops) and later popes lacked the zeal to reform.

As a result of these serious problems, the Protestant Reformation began when Martin Luther, an Augustinian monk and professor of Scripture in Wittenberg, Germany, posted his Ninety-five Theses on Indulgences in 1517. Although Luther initially had no intention of leaving the Catholic Church, when his cries for reform went unheeded, the German nobility and people responded by forming the "Lutheran" Church, with the Bible alone as their guide in doctrine and the belief in justification by faith alone. The followers of Luther retained many Catholic practices and beliefs, but later reforming groups, such as those led by Jean Calvin in Geneva, Switzerland, Huldreich Zwingli in Zurich and the Anabaptists, in turn rejected more radically the heritage and tradition of Catholicism.

The Catholic Church in the sixteenth century responded by seeking to reform itself and to counter these Protestant groups. Even before Luther, Catholic humanist scholars led by Erasmus of Rotterdam were appealing for reform. The vanguard of the Catholic Reformation became the Society of Jesus (the Jesuits) founded by Spaniard Saint Ignatius of Loyola. Other new Catholic religious orders of men and women emerged, and old orders were reformed.

Catholic identity was bolstered by the Council of Trent (1545–1563), which defined Catholic doctrine, tightened discipline and established the seminary system to provide for holy, educated priests. Reforming popes and bishops became the rule, not the exception, and many great saints emerged: Philip Neri, "second apostle of Rome" and leader of the Roman Oratory; Jesuit missionaries Saint Francis Xavier (the Far East), Saint Jean de Brebeuf and Saint Isaac Jogues (North America); Spanish mystics Saint Teresa of Avila and Saint John of the Cross (both of the Carmelite Order); Jesuit theologians Saint Peter Canisius and Saint Robert Bellarmine; bishops Saint Charles Borromeo and Saint Francis de Sales; religious foundress Saint Jeanne de Chantal and champion of the poor Saint Vincent de Paul. Out of the depths of its many problems in the late fifteenth century, the Catholic Church, by the grace of God, returned once again to strength and virtue marked by discipline, devotion and clear doctrine.

CHAPTER FIVE

The Catholic Church Confronts the Modern World
(AD 1650–1900)

The period from 1650 to the present is often termed the modern era. It is marked by the emergence of science and technology, a new philosophy based primarily on reason (though later including a fuller range of human experience), the demise of the idea of the divine right of kings to rule and the increasing exclusion of religion from the public life of society.

The earliest stage of this modern era is often termed the Enlightenment because of the rise of science and philosophies based solely on reason. Religion was thought to divide mankind, whereas reason was thought to bring unity. French mathematician Blaise Pascal, Anglican bishop Joseph Butler and others sought to reassert the truth of Christian revelation. The Catholic Church's condemnation of Galileo was thought to signify a total opposition to modern science, but in many ways the Catholic faith gave rise to science.

France is representative of the crisis of the Catholic Church in Europe from 1650 to 1800. Absolutist rulers, such as Louis XIV, and popular sentiment called for a decreased influence of the Church in public affairs and even for a national church freed from the control of Rome. Confusion about Catholic teaching and spirituality was manifested in the strict Jansenist movement and the passive, spiritual Quietists.

The strongest opponents to such movements were the controversial Jesuits. But the popes were pressured into suppressing the Society of Jesus, first in France and then worldwide (except Russia) in 1773.

The weakened condition of the Catholic Church was shown most starkly by the French Revolution (1789), which went so far as to abolish Christianity altogether and to set up instead a religion of reason and then the cult of the supreme being. Western civilization was shocked by all of this and took a more conservative stance in the beginning of the nineteenth century.

The nineteenth century began with a reaction against the excesses of the French Revolution, but the movement for representative governments granting freedom of speech, the press, conscience and religion steadily grew. Along with this political liberalism, there was a desire among intellectuals for new methods of historical and literary criticism to be applied to the

Bible and for a fresh look at traditional Christian theology.

The Catholic Church generally stood against these innovations, arguing that only the true faith should have rights and fearing the erosion of the authority of the Bible and the Church in people's lives. Pope Pius IX condemned the modern trends in his Syllabus of Errors (1864), and the First Vatican Council (1869–1870) affirmed the primacy of faith over reason and defined the teaching infallibility of the pope in certain clearly defined instances. He also defined the doctrine of the Immaculate Conception of Mary in 1854.

Although the political influence of the papacy waned, the pope's spiritual authority was greatly enhanced in the nineteenth century. Pope Leo XIII continued this strong leadership but carried on more of a dialogue with the modern world. He published the first great Catholic encyclical letter on the economic and social order, *Rerum Novarum* (1891).

CHAPTER SIX

The Catholic Church in the Twentieth Century
(AD 1900–1963)

The twentieth century was a time of rapid change, especially brought about by science and technology. In spite of advances in these areas, mankind apparently had not grown in wisdom and morality. More people were killed in warfare in this century than ever before, and the world stood on the brink of nuclear holocaust.

Ideologies competed for people's allegiance and divided the world: Fascism and Nazism against the democracies; communism against capitalism; poor nations against rich nations. Secular humanism and materialism sapped the strength of Christianity in the Western world, while communism suppressed the faith in much of the East. And yet, where sin abounds, God's grace abounds even more (see Romans 5:20).

Pope Saint Pius X was leader of the Catholic Church from 1903 to 1914. He worked vigorously to strengthen Catholic worship and teaching and to protect the Catholic Church against modern errors. He called for the codification of canon law, which was completed in 1917. His condemnation of Modernism (the use of modern historical and biblical scholarship, which led to a denial of certain truths of faith) was very severe but probably saved the Catholic Church from the division that split Protestantism into two camps, liberal and fundamentalist.

The Great War (World War I) occupied the time and attention of Pope Benedict XV (1914–1922) and of most of the Western world. The pope strove to maintain the strict neutrality of the Church and to reconcile the warring parties. Nineteen-seventeen marked both the beginning of the communist rule of Russia and the appearances of Mary in Fatima, Portugal, in which Mary exhorted all Christians to repentance and prayer, especially for the conversion of Russia.

Pope Pius XI (1922–1939) scathingly condemned communism in 1937 but had to contend with the growing threat of the totalitarian regimes of Mussolini in Italy and Adolf Hitler in Germany. Pius XI signed concordats with these and other nations to preserve the freedom of Catholics in their realms, but he did not hesitate to condemn Fascism and Nazism in his fiery encyclical of 1937, *Mit Brennender Sorge*. His establishment of the Feast of Christ the King in 1925 proclaimed Christ's kingship over the world, and he spelled out further the social and economic implications of this in the encyclical *Quadragesimo Anno* (1931). The Catholic Action movement permeated the world with the gospel spirit.

Pope Pius XII (1939–1958) faced the reality of another world war and worked tirelessly behind the scenes to save the lives of hundreds of thousands of Jews. This pope also began to open the Catholic Church to new methods of scholarship and biblical criticism (*Divino Afflante Spiritu*, 1943) and to new ways of looking at the Church. He called it the mystical body of Christ in his encyclical of this name, which began to break down the image of the Catholic Church as an unchanging fortress opposed to the modern world. He increased the number of non-Italian cardinals, emphasizing the universality of the Catholic Church. He strongly opposed communism and encouraged Catholics to seek the intercession of Mary. He defined (infallibly) in 1950 the doctrine of Mary's bodily assumption into heaven.

CHAPTER SEVEN

The Second Vatican Council to Pope Benedict XVI

The Second Vatican Council (1962–1965) was a landmark event for the Catholic Church, defining itself and its relationship to the modern world. Pope John XXIII (1958–1963) called the council to renew the Church and to bring it up-to-date *(aggiornamento)*—still maintaining its eternal truth and continuity with the past. While the First Vatican Council emphasized the importance and role of the pope, the Second Vatican Council completed this by defining the role of the bishops, priests, religious and laypeople as well. The Dogmatic

Constitution on the Church *(Lumen Gentium)* provides the basis for this and gives an overall understanding on the Church as a mystery and as the people of God.

The Second Vatican Council also opened the door to Catholic participation in restoring the unity of Christianity through its Decree on Ecumenism. The Declaration on Non-Christian Religions gave a positive impetus to Catholics' relations to Jews and other non-Christians. The right of all people to freely exercise their beliefs was affirmed in the Declaration on Religious Freedom.

Other major documents of Vatican II were the Dogmatic Constitution on Divine Revelation and the council's longest document, the Pastoral Constitution on the Church in the Modern World *(Gaudium et Spes)*. This latter constitution set forth general principles for Catholic attitudes toward the modern world and presented guidelines for approaching specific areas of concern today. The Constitution on the Sacred Liturgy had the most immediate direct impact on the daily lives of Catholics. Along with other liturgical reforms, Mass could now be celebrated in the language of the people.

Overall the Second Vatican Council had tremendous positive impact and appeared to fulfill Pope John XXIII's prayer for a "new Pentecost" in the Catholic Church.

Who was this remarkable man, John XXIII, who called for the Second Vatican Council? In 1958 he was an affable seventy-six-year-old cardinal who was supposed to be an interim pope, a compromise candidate. He attributed his calling the Second Vatican Council to an inspiration of the Holy Spirit. John XXIII did not allow the council to repeat old formulations of

Catholic doctrine but insisted on a fresh restatement of the Catholic tradition that would speak to the modern world.

Pope John XXIII also promulgated important encyclicals on the social order *(Mater et Magistra)* and peace in the world *(Pacem in Terris)*, which also spoke to modern man. This universally beloved pope died suddenly after the first session of his council.

The man who had the critical task of teaching the Catholic Church while completing the Second Vatican Council and implementing it was Pope Paul VI (1963–1978). He fostered the revolutionary work of the council but saw the importance of implementing it gradually.

In spite of Pope Paul's efforts at moderation, the Catholic Church underwent one of its most unsettled periods. Genuine movements of renewal existed alongside irresponsible experimentation. Some Catholics interpreted the council in distorted ways, and many priests and religious abandoned their vocations when discipline was loosened and contact with the modern world was encouraged.

However, none of this outweighs the positive accomplishments of Vatican II. Overall the condition of the Catholic Church would have been much more serious had Vatican II not opened the Church to the modern world. Pope Paul VI gave wise guidance in this difficult period.

Pope John Paul I died only thirty-three days after his election in 1978, and his successor, John Paul II, was the first Polish pope and the first non-Italian pope since the sixteenth century. Pope John Paul II was totally dedicated to advancing the principles of Vatican II, while cautioning against possible abuses. His encyclicals stressed the primacy of Christ *(Redemptor Hominis)*, the mercy of God *(Dives in Misericordia)* and the rights and dignity of workers *(Laborem Exercens)*. The dignity of the human person and the defense of orthodox Catholic teaching were key themes of his papacy.

John Paul II was most prominent as an apostle spreading the good news of Jesus Christ throughout the world, including building ecumenical relations. He traveled more extensively than any previous pope, in spite of an assassination attempt that nearly took his life.

Pope Benedict XVI, a German-born theologian, became pope after serving as prefect of the Sacred Congregation for the Doctrine of the Faith for twenty-four years (1981–2005) under Pope John Paul II. Known for the profound insight of his teaching, he began his pontificate stressing the quest for Christian unity and interreligious dialogue, the beauty and solemnity of the Latin liturgy and, above all, a message for hope for the human race based on its Savior, Jesus Christ. Though different in personality and style from John Paul II, Pope Benedict XVI has expressed his desire to continue to promote the renewal of the Church, according to the authentic norms of the Second Vatican Council, and the "new evangelization," by confronting the modern "dictatorship of relativism" with the eternal truth of the gospel.

CHAPTER EIGHT

A Perspective on Church History and on the Role of Mary
Chapter eight is a summary and conclusion to the preceding seven chapters, showing that the history of the Catholic Church is continually marked by renewals brought about by the power of God's Holy Spirit. In spite of periods of struggle

and decline, Jesus' promise to remain with the Church until the end of time (see Matthew 28:20) is shown by the continual surges of reform and renewal that have followed times of difficulty. Although the Church is made up of sinners, its history is full of great saints, heroic men and women who have boldly witnessed to their faith in Jesus Christ, often with their lives.

The role of Mary as Mother of the Church, model of the Church and God's messenger to the Church through her apparitions (appearances) is also discussed. As the final chapter of Vatican II's Dogmatic Constitution on the Church explains, Mary continues to have a motherly care as a powerful intercessor for the Church. She is also to be imitated by all the other Church's members as the exemplary disciple or follower of her Son, Jesus Christ.

It also appears, though Catholics are not required to believe this, that Mary has come at various times in the Church's history to bring a particular message or word of God for that particular age or people, much as the angels were God's messengers in the Old Testament. Today the message particularly important for Catholics is the message of repentance, conversion and prayer given by Our Lady of Fatima in 1917. Other reported appearances of Mary have occurred since, confirming the message of Fatima and attesting to the basic gospel of Jesus Christ.

PREFACE

1. The ICCRO serves the worldwide charismatic renewal in various ways. While making no claim of authority for directly supervising the renewal—in every area of the world where Catholic charismatic renewal exists, it is always subject to the authority of the local ordinary—the office attempts to assure the pastoral and theological soundness of renewal groups everywhere. Its basic goals are to be a center for information regarding the development and activities of the renewal; to organize international leadership conferences; to sponsor training programs; and to serve as a center of unity for the renewal both within the Church and with all elements of renewal throughout the world.

   The Life in the Spirit Seminar is a series of teachings that promote understanding of and openness to the Holy Spirit and his gifts and introduce people to charismatic renewal.

ONE

The Catholic Understanding of the Church

1. Cardinal Leon Joseph Suenens, Address to the International Conference on Catholic Charismatic Renewal, University of Notre Dame, June 15, 1974.
2. Ignatius of Antioch, Letter to the Smyrnaeans, 8:2, in Cyril C. Richardson, ed., *Early Christian Fathers* (New York: MacMillan, 1970), p. 115.
3. Augustine, *Confessions*, bk. 9, chap. 10, no. 26, in Henry Chadwick, trans., *Oxford World Classics* (New York: Oxford University Press, 1998), p. 172.

TWO

The Church of the Apostles and the Fathers (AD 50–600)

1. Attributed to Tertullian. See Henry Chadwick, *The Early Church* (New York: Penguin, 1990), p. 56; Anthony Gilles, *The People of the Creed* (Cincinnati: St. Anthony Messenger Press, 1985), p. 51.

2. Tertullian, *Apologeticus*, chap. 50.

3. Irenaeus of Lyons, "Refutation and Overthrow of the Knowledge Falsely So-Called," *Against Heresies*, bk. 3, 3:2, in Richardson, p. 372.

4. Cyprian of Carthage, "Letter to Antonian," chapter 1 in *St. Cyprian Letters* (1–81), *Fathers of the Church* series, vol. 51 (Washington, D.C.: Catholic University Press, 1964), p. 134.

5. Jerome, "Dialogue Against the Luciferians," no. 19, in W.H. Fremantle, trans., *St. Jerome: Letters and Selected Works*, vol. 6 of *Nicene and Post-Nicene Fathers*, second series (Peabody, Mass.: Hendrickson, 1994), p. 329.

6. Ambrose, *Commentary on Twelve Psalms of David* 40:30 (AD 389).

7. Jerome, Letters, 15:2, quoted in Michael Schmaus, *The Church: Its Origins and Structures*, vol. 4 of *Dogma* (Westminster, Md.: Christian Classics, 1984), p. 184.

8. Alfred Lapple, *The Catholic Church: A Brief History*, Peter Heinegg, trans. (New York: Paulist, 1982), p. 34. (Originally published in 1982 as *Kirchenoeschichte Impulse Zur Kurskorekter* by Don Bosco Verlag, Munich.)

THREE

The Church of the Middle Ages (AD 600–1300)

1. Pope Gregory I wrote to Serenus, bishop of Marseilles, "For pictorial representation is made use of in the Church for this reason: that such as are ignorant of letters may at least read by looking at the walls what they cannot read in books" (James Barnby, trans., Epistle 60, *Nicene and Post-Nicene Fathers*, second series, vol. 13 [Peabody, Mass.: Hendrickson, 1994], p. 23).

2. Pope Gregory VII, quoted in Christopher Dawson, *The Historic Reality of Christian Culture* (New York: Harper, 1960), p. 54.

3. Steven Runciman, *A History of the Crusades,* vol. 3 (New York: Penguin, 1978), p. 123.

FOUR

The Late Middle Ages, Reformation and Counter-Reformation (AD 1300–1650)

1. Quoted in William R. Estep, *Renaissance and Reformation* (Grand Rapids, Mich.: Eerdmans, 1986), p. 119.

2. Owen Chadwick, *The Reformation* (Baltimore: Penguin, 1972), p. 22.

3. Quoted in Chadwick, p. 91.

4. Thomas Bokenkotter, *A Concise History of the Catholic Church* (Garden City, N.J.: Doubleday, 1979), pp. 262–263.

FIVE

The Catholic Church Confronts the Modern World (AD 1650–1900)

1. Immanuel Kant, "What Is Enlightenment?" in Lewis White Beck, *Kant: Selections* (New York: Macmillan, 1988), p. 462.

2. Lapple, p. 70.

SIX

The Catholic Church in the Twentieth Century (AD 1900–1963)

1. Pope John Paul II, Apostolic Letter *Novo Millennio Ineunte*, no. 57 (Boston: Pauline, 2001), p. 74.

2. John D. Delaney, ed., *A Woman Clothed With the Sun* (New York: Doubleday, 1961), p. 194.

3. Pope Leo XIII, *Quod Apostolici Muneris*, December 28, 1878, no. 1.

4. Pinchas E. Lapide, *The Last Three Popes and the Jews*, as reported by George Murphy, *Democrat and Chronicle*, Rochester, N.Y., June 14, 1981, p. 8B, col. 2.

5. Heinrich Himmler, in a letter to Reinhard Heidrich, as reported by Murphy, p. 8B, cols. 1 and 2.

6. Pope John XXIII, *Humanae Salutis*, Apostolic Constitution Convoking the Council, December 25, 1961, in Walter Abbott, S.J., ed., *Documents of Vatican II* (Piscataway, N.J.: New Century, 1966), p. 709.

7. Bokenkotter, p. 413.

SEVEN

The Second Vatican Council to Pope Benedict XVI

1. *Novo Millennio Ineunte*, no. 57, p. 74.

2. *Dei Verbum*, no. 13, in Austin Flannery, ed., *Vatican Council II: The Conciliar and Post Conciliar Documents* (Northport, N.Y.: Costello, 1996), vol. 1, p. 758.

3. *Dei Verbum*, no. 25, in Flannery, p. 764.

4. Vatican Council II, *Unitatis Redintegratio*, no. 11, in Abbot, p. 364.

5. Cardinal Joseph Ratzinger with Vittorio Messori, *The Ratzinger Report: An Exclusive Interview on the State of the Church* (San Francisco: Ignatius, 1985), p. 43.

6. *Novo Millennio Ineunte*, no. 57, p. 74.

7. *Novo Millennio Ineunte*, no. 58, p. 75.

8. First homily of His Holiness Benedict XVI at the end of the eucharistic concelebration with the cardinal electors in the Sistine Chapel, April 20, 2005.

9. Homily of His Holiness Benedict XVI in St. Patrick: Cathedral, New York City, April 19, 2008.

10. *Ratzinger Report*, p. 43.

EIGHT

A Perspective on Church History and on the Role of Mary

1. Karl Adam, *The Spirit of Catholicism* (Garden City, N.J.: Doubleday, 1954), pp. 6–7.

2. Christopher Dawson, "The Six Ages of the Church," *The Historic Reality of Christian Culture* (New York: Harper, 1960), p. 47.

3. The Second Vatican Council, "Dogmatic Constitution on the Church," no. 62, in Abbot, p. 91.

4. Gerald J. Farrell and George W. Kosicki, *The Spirit and the Bride Say "Come"!: Mary's Role in the New Pentecost* (Asbury, N.J.: AMI, 1981), pp. 53–54.

5. Delaney, p. 137.

6. Farrell and Kosicki, pp. 51–52.

7. Farrell and Kosicki, pp. 51–52.

8. Quoted in *Ratzinger Report*, p. 110.

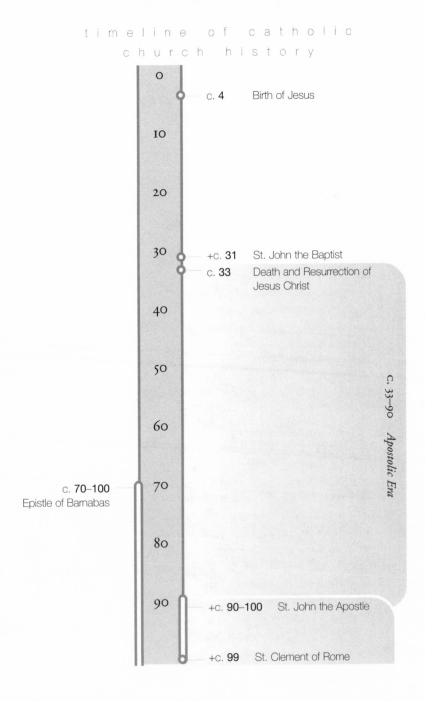

0

c. **4**   Birth of Jesus

10

20

30   +c. **31**   St. John the Baptist

c. **33**   Death and Resurrection of
Jesus Christ

40

50

60

c. **70–100**   70
Epistle of Barnabas

c. 33–90   Apostolic Era

80

90   +c. **90–100**   St. John the Apostle

+c. **99**   St. Clement of Rome

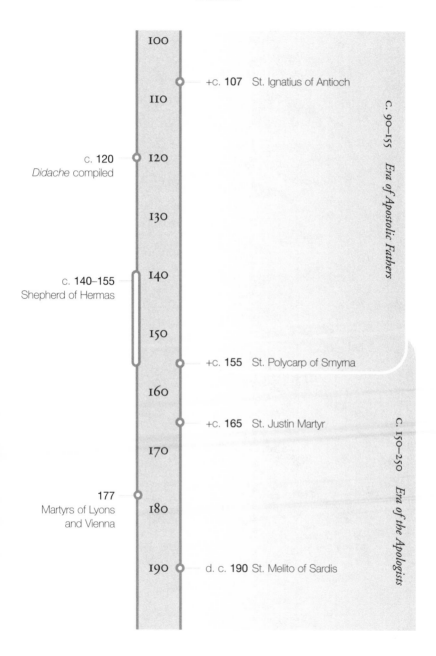

100

+c. **107** St. Ignatius of Antioch

110

c. **120**
Didache compiled

120

130

c. **140–155**
Shepherd of Hermas

140

150

+c. **155** St. Polycarp of Smyrna

160

+c. **165** St. Justin Martyr

170

177
Martyrs of Lyons
and Vienna

180

190   d. c. **190** St. Melito of Sardis

c. 90–155 *Era of Apostolic Fathers*

c. 150–250 *Era of the Apologists*

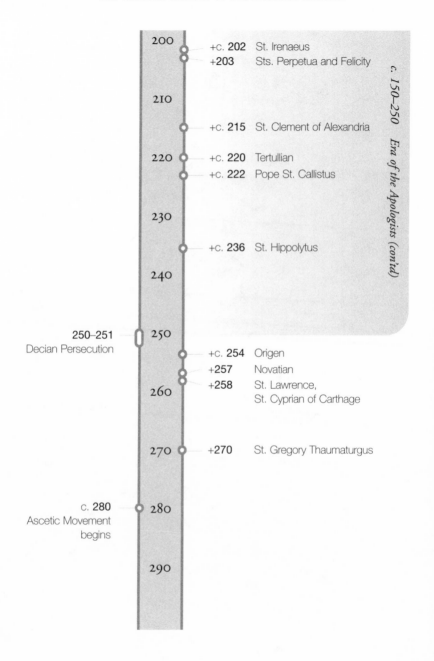

200

+c. 202 St. Irenaeus
+203 Sts. Perpetua and Felicity

210

+c. 215 St. Clement of Alexandria

220 +c. 220 Tertullian
+c. 222 Pope St. Callistus

230

+c. 236 St. Hippolytus

240

250–251
Decian Persecution

250

+c. 254 Origen
+257 Novatian
+258 St. Lawrence,
St. Cyprian of Carthage

260

270 +270 St. Gregory Thaumaturgus

c. 280
Ascetic Movement
begins

280

290

c. 150–250 Era of the Apologists (con'd)

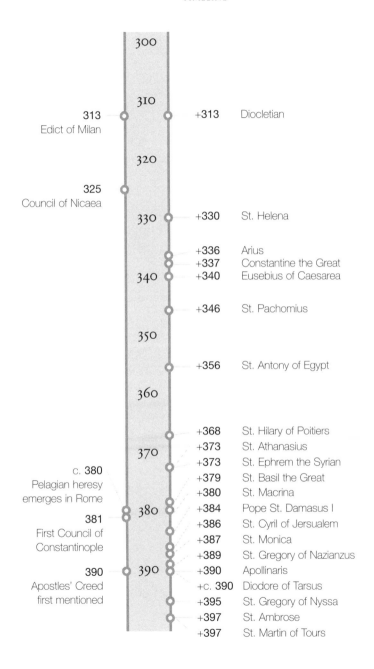

300

310

313
Edict of Milan

+313   Diocletian

320

325
Council of Nicaea

330   +330   St. Helena

+336   Arius
+337   Constantine the Great
340   +340   Eusebius of Caesarea

+346   St. Pachomius

350

+356   St. Antony of Egypt

360

+368   St. Hilary of Poitiers
+373   St. Athanasius
370   +373   St. Ephrem the Syrian
c. 380   +379   St. Basil the Great
Pelagian heresy   +380   St. Macrina
emerges in Rome
+384   Pope St. Damasus I
381   +386   St. Cyril of Jersualem
First Council of   +387   St. Monica
Constantinople
+389   St. Gregory of Nazianzus
390   390   +390   Apollinaris
Apostles' Creed   +c. 390   Diodore of Tarsus
first mentioned   +395   St. Gregory of Nyssa
+397   St. Ambrose
+397   St. Martin of Tours

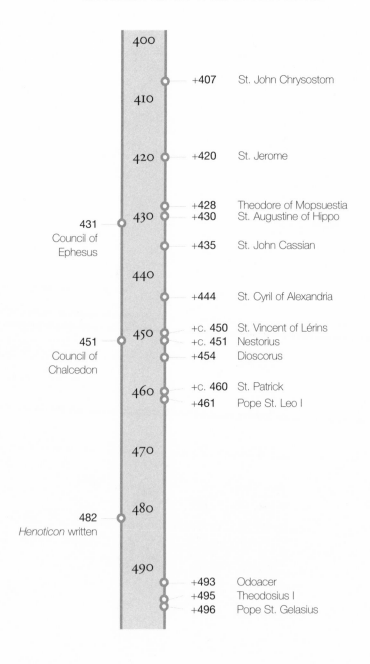

400

+407   St. John Chrysostom

410

420   +420   St. Jerome

+428   Theodore of Mopsuestia
430   +430   St. Augustine of Hippo

431
Council of
Ephesus

+435   St. John Cassian

440

+444   St. Cyril of Alexandria

+c. 450   St. Vincent of Lérins
450   +c. 451   Nestorius

451
Council of
Chalcedon

+454   Dioscorus

+c. 460   St. Patrick
460   +461   Pope St. Leo I

470

482
Henoticon written

480

490

+493   Odoacer
+495   Theodosius I
+496   Pope St. Gelasius

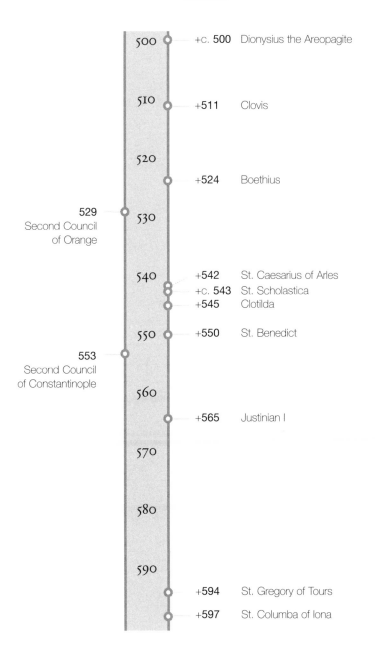

500

+c. 500 — Dionysius the Areopagite

510

+511 — Clovis

520

+524 — Boethius

529
Second Council
of Orange

530

540

+542 — St. Caesarius of Arles
+c. 543 — St. Scholastica
+545 — Clotilda

550

+550 — St. Benedict

553
Second Council
of Constantinople

560

+565 — Justinian I

570

580

590

+594 — St. Gregory of Tours

+597 — St. Columba of Iona

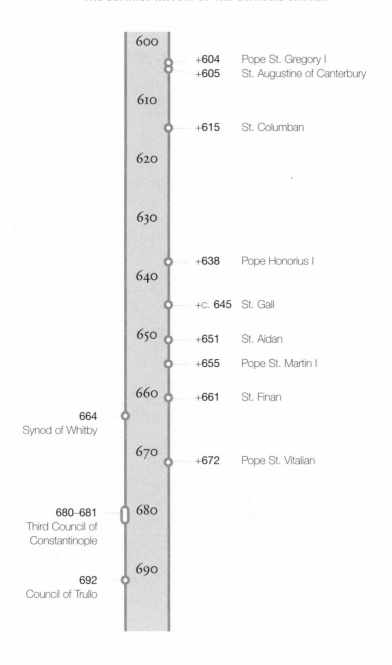

600

+604   Pope St. Gregory I
+605   St. Augustine of Canterbury

610

+615   St. Columban

620

630

+638   Pope Honorius I

640

+c. 645   St. Gall

650   +651   St. Aidan

+655   Pope St. Martin I

660   +661   St. Finan

664
Synod of Whitby

670   +672   Pope St. Vitalian

680–681   680
Third Council of
Constantinople

690

692
Council of Trullo

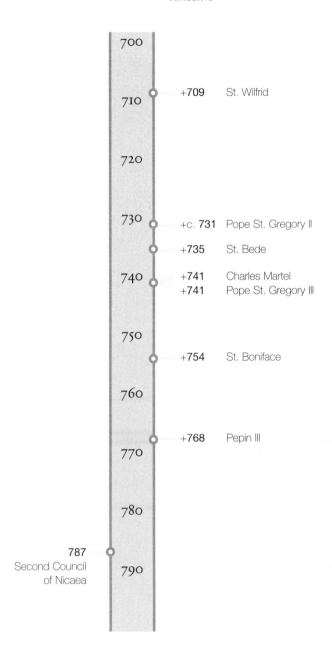

700

+709   St. Wilfrid
710

720

730   +c. 731   Pope St. Gregory II

+735   St. Bede

740   +741   Charles Martel
+741   Pope St. Gregory III

750

+754   St. Boniface

760

+768   Pepin III
770

780

787
Second Council   790
of Nicaea

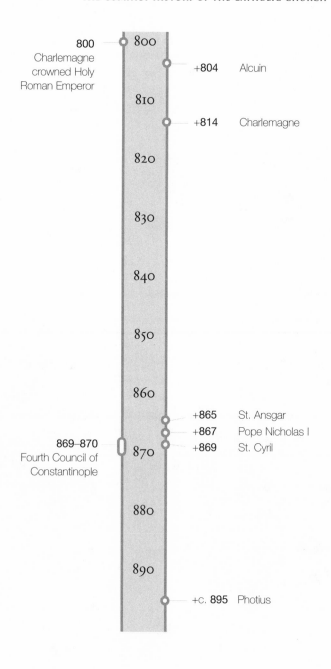

800
Charlemagne
crowned Holy
Roman Emperor

800

+804   Alcuin

810

+814   Charlemagne

820

830

840

850

860

+865   St. Ansgar
+867   Pope Nicholas I

869–870
Fourth Council of
Constantinople

870

+869   St. Cyril

880

890

+c. **895**   Photius

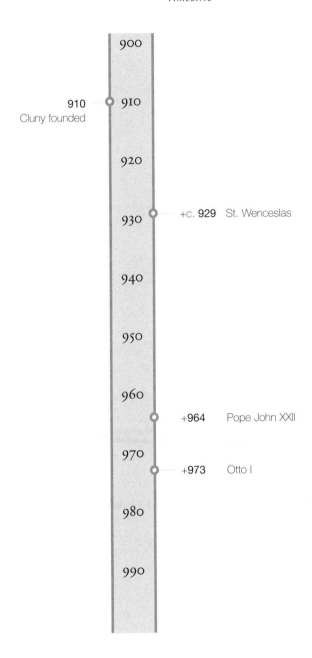

900

910
910 Cluny founded

920

930 +c. 929 St. Wenceslas

940

950

960 +964 Pope John XXII

970 +973 Otto I

980

990

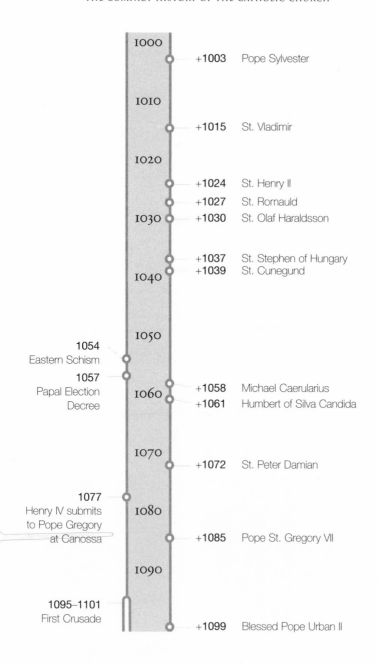

1000

+1003   Pope Sylvester

1010

+1015   St. Vladimir

1020

+1024   St. Henry II
+1027   St. Romauld
1030 +1030   St. Olaf Haraldsson

+1037   St. Stephen of Hungary
1040 +1039   St. Cunegund

1050

1054
Eastern Schism

1057
Papal Election 1060
Decree

+1058   Michael Caerularius
+1061   Humbert of Silva Candida

1070

+1072   St. Peter Damian

1077
Henry IV submits
to Pope Gregory 1080
at Canossa

+1085   Pope St. Gregory VII

1090

1095–1101
First Crusade

+1099   Blessed Pope Urban II

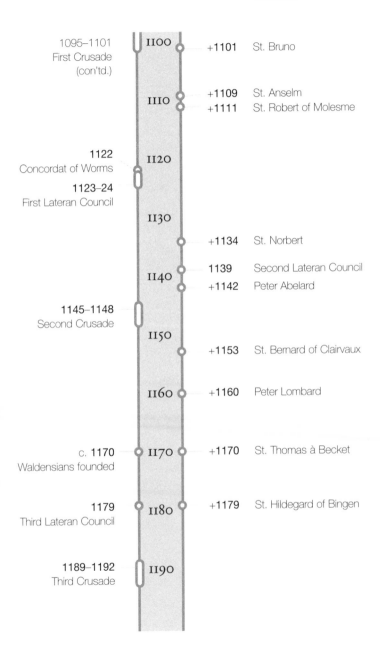

1095–1101 First Crusade (con'td.)	**1100**	**+1101** St. Bruno
	1110	**+1109** St. Anselm
		+1111 St. Robert of Molesme
1122 Concordat of Worms	**1120**	
1123–24 First Lateran Council		
	1130	
		+1134 St. Norbert
	1140	**1139** Second Lateran Council
		+1142 Peter Abelard
1145–1148 Second Crusade	**1150**	
		+1153 St. Bernard of Clairvaux
	1160	**+1160** Peter Lombard
c. **1170** Waldensians founded	**1170**	**+1170** St. Thomas à Becket
1179 Third Lateran Council	**1180**	**+1179** St. Hildegard of Bingen
1189–1192 Third Crusade	**1190**	

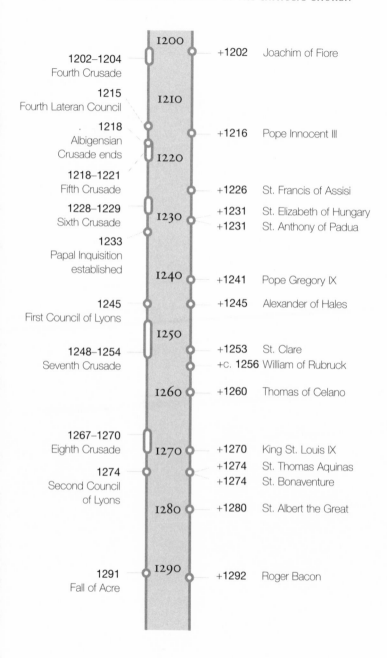

1200

1202–1204
Fourth Crusade

+1202   Joachim of Fiore

1215
Fourth Lateran Council

1210

1218
Albigensian
Crusade ends

+1216   Pope Innocent III

1220

1218–1221
Fifth Crusade

+1226   St. Francis of Assisi

1228–1229
Sixth Crusade

1230

+1231   St. Elizabeth of Hungary
+1231   St. Anthony of Padua

1233
Papal Inquisition
established

1240

+1241   Pope Gregory IX

1245
First Council of Lyons

+1245   Alexander of Hales

1250

1248–1254
Seventh Crusade

+1253   St. Clare
+c. **1256** William of Rubruck

1260

+1260   Thomas of Celano

1267–1270
Eighth Crusade

1270

+1270   King St. Louis IX

1274
Second Council
of Lyons

+1274   St. Thomas Aquinas
+1274   St. Bonaventure

1280

+1280   St. Albert the Great

1291
Fall of Acre

1290

+1292   Roger Bacon

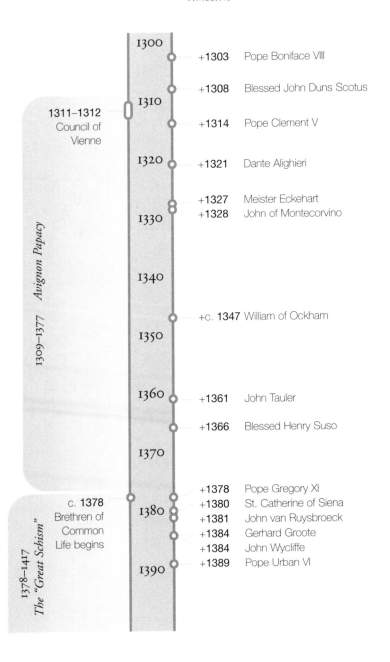

1300

+1303   Pope Boniface VIII

+1308   Blessed John Duns Scotus

1311–1312
Council of
Vienne

1310

+1314   Pope Clement V

1320

+1321   Dante Alighieri

+1327   Meister Eckehart
+1328   John of Montecorvino

1330

1340

+c. 1347 William of Ockham

1350

Avignon Papacy

1309–1377

1360

+1361   John Tauler

+1366   Blessed Henry Suso

1370

c. 1378
Brethren of
Common
Life begins

1378

1380

+1378   Pope Gregory XI
+1380   St. Catherine of Siena
+1381   John van Ruysbroeck
+1384   Gerhard Groote
+1384   John Wycliffe
+1389   Pope Urban VI

The "Great Schism"

1378–1417

1390

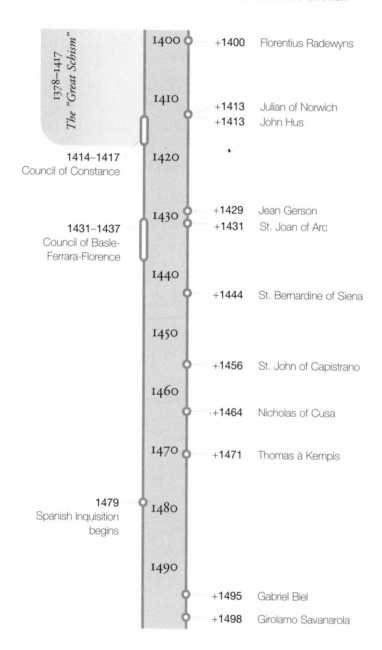

1378–1417
The "Great Schism"

1414–1417
Council of Constance

1431–1437
Council of Basle-
Ferrara-Florence

1479
Spanish Inquisition
begins

1400

1410

1420

1430

1440

1450

1460

1470

1480

1490

+1400   Florentius Radewyns

+1413   Julian of Norwich
+1413   John Hus

+1429   Jean Gerson
+1431   St. Joan of Arc

+1444   St. Bernardine of Siena

+1456   St. John of Capistrano

+1464   Nicholas of Cusa

+1471   Thomas à Kempis

+1495   Gabriel Biel
+1498   Girolamo Savanarola

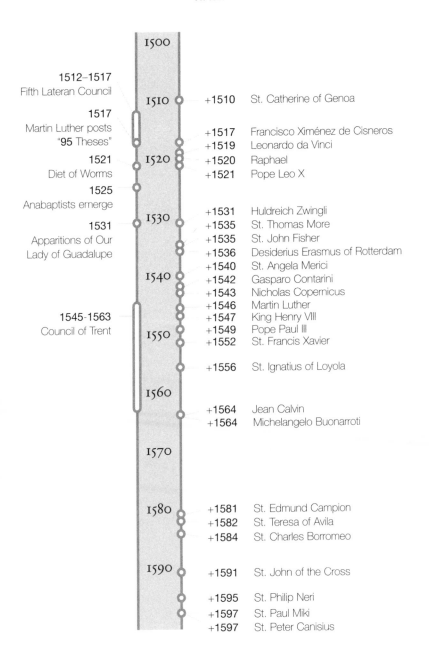

1500

1512–1517
Fifth Lateran Council

1510   +1510   St. Catherine of Genoa

1517
Martin Luther posts
"95 Theses"
                +1517   Francisco Ximénez de Cisneros
                +1519   Leonardo da Vinci

1521   **1520**   +1520   Raphael
Diet of Worms   +1521   Pope Leo X

1525
Anabaptists emerge
                +1531   Huldreich Zwingli
1530   +1535   St. Thomas More
1531   +1535   St. John Fisher
Apparitions of Our
Lady of Guadalupe   +1536   Desiderius Erasmus of Rotterdam
                +1540   St. Angela Merici
1540   +1542   Gasparo Contarini
                +1543   Nicholas Copernicus
                +1546   Martin Luther
1545-1563   +1547   King Henry VIII
Council of Trent   +1549   Pope Paul III
1550   +1552   St. Francis Xavier

                +1556   St. Ignatius of Loyola

1560
                +1564   Jean Calvin
                +1564   Michelangelo Buonarroti

1570

1580   +1581   St. Edmund Campion
                +1582   St. Teresa of Avila
                +1584   St. Charles Borromeo

1590   +1591   St. John of the Cross

                +1595   St. Philip Neri

                +1597   St. Paul Miki
                +1597   St. Peter Canisius

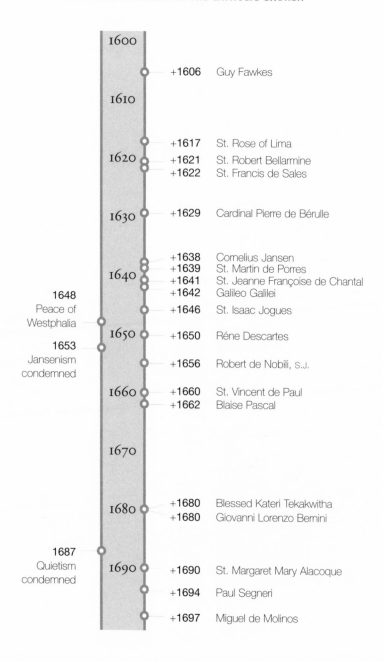

1600

+1606 Guy Fawkes

1610

+1617 St. Rose of Lima
1620 +1621 St. Robert Bellarmine
+1622 St. Francis de Sales

1630 +1629 Cardinal Pierre de Bérulle

+1638 Cornelius Jansen
+1639 St. Martin de Porres
1640 +1641 St. Jeanne Françoise de Chantal
+1642 Galileo Galilei

+1646 St. Isaac Jogues

1648
Peace of
Westphalia
1650 +1650 Réne Descartes

1653
Jansenism
condemned

+1656 Robert de Nobili, S.J.

1660 +1660 St. Vincent de Paul
+1662 Blaise Pascal

1670

1680 +1680 Blessed Kateri Tekakwitha
+1680 Giovanni Lorenzo Bernini

1687
Quietism
condemned
1690 +1690 St. Margaret Mary Alacoque

+1694 Paul Segneri

+1697 Miguel de Molinos

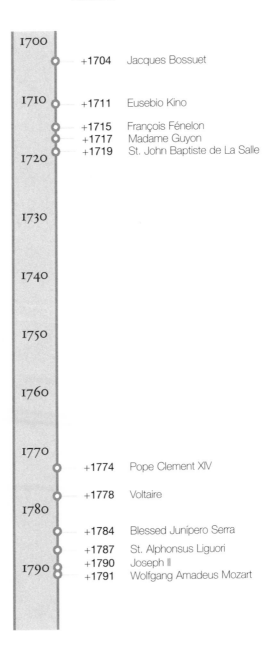

1700		
	+1704	Jacques Bossuet
1710	+1711	Eusebio Kino
	+1715	François Fénelon
	+1717	Madame Guyon
1720	+1719	St. John Baptiste de La Salle
1730		
1740		
1750		
1760		
1770		
	+1774	Pope Clement XIV
	+1778	Voltaire
1780		
	+1784	Blessed Junípero Serra
	+1787	St. Alphonsus Liguori
	+1790	Joseph II
1790	+1791	Wolfgang Amadeus Mozart

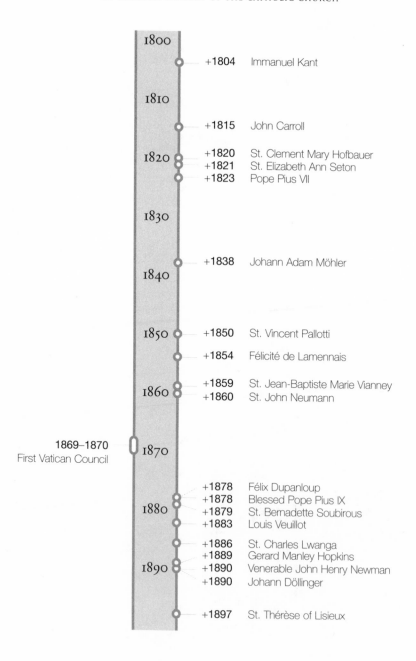

1800

+1804   Immanuel Kant

1810

+1815   John Carroll

1820   +1820   St. Clement Mary Hofbauer
         +1821   St. Elizabeth Ann Seton
         +1823   Pope Pius VII

1830

+1838   Johann Adam Möhler

1840

1850   +1850   St. Vincent Pallotti

+1854   Félicité de Lamennais

+1859   St. Jean-Baptiste Marie Vianney
1860   +1860   St. John Neumann

1869–1870   1870
First Vatican Council

+1878   Félix Dupanloup
+1878   Blessed Pope Pius IX
1880   +1879   St. Bernadette Soubirous
+1883   Louis Veuillot

+1886   St. Charles Lwanga
+1889   Gerard Manley Hopkins
1890   +1890   Venerable John Henry Newman
+1890   Johann Döllinger

+1897   St. Thérèse of Lisieux

1900	
	+1902 St. Maria Goretti
	+1902 Lord Acton
	+1903 Pope Leo XIII
1910	
	+1914 Pope St. Pius X
+1917 Apparitions of Our Lady of Fatima	+1917 St. Frances Xavier Cabrini
1920	
+1943 Chiara Lubich founds "Focolare"	+1925 Friedrich von Hügel
+1945 Cursillo founded	
1930	
+1948 World Council of Churches	+1936 G.K. Chesterton
	+1939 Pope Pius XI
1940	+1940 Alfred Loisy
1954 "Communion and Liberation" founded by Luigi Giussani	+1941 St. Maximilian Kolbe
	+1942 St. Edith Stein
1950	+1949 Maurice Blondel
1962–1965 Second Vatican Council	+1955 Pierre Teilhard de Chardin
1967 Catholic Pentecostal Movement begins	
1960	+1963 Blessed Pope John XXIII
	+1966 Karl Adam
1968 Pope Paul VI issues *Humanae Vitae*	+1967 John Courtney Murray
	+1967 Francis Joseph Spellman
1970	+1968 Thomas Merton
1978 John Paul II elected pope	+1975 St. Josemaría Escrívá
	+1978 Pope Paul VI
	+1979 Fulton J. Sheen
1980	+1980 Oscar Romero
1981 Cardinal Joseph Ratzinger made prefect of Congregation for the Doctrine of the Faith	+1980 Servant of God Dorothy Day
	+1984 Bernard Lonergan
	+1984 Karl Rahner
	+1988 Hans Urs von Balthasar
1990	+1991 Henri de Lubac
	+1995 Marie-Joseph Yves Congar
	+1996 Leon Joseph Suenens
1984 Pope John Paul II holds first World Youth Day	+1997 Mother Teresa of Calcutta
	+1999 Helder Camara

2000
The Great Jubilee Year

2000
Pope John Paul II
canonizes St. Faustina
and establishes Divine
Mercy Sunday

2001
Pope John Paul II
issues *Novo
Millennio Ineunte*

2005
Election of Pope
Benedict XVI

2005
Year of the Eucharist

2006
Pope Benedict XVI
address, "Faith,
Reason and the
University Memories
& Reflections"

2008
Pope Benedict XVI's
Apostolic Journey to
the United States

2000

2010

2020

2030

2040

2050

2060

2070

2080

2090

+2005 Pope John Paul II
2007 *Jesus of Nazareth*, first book published by Benedict XVI as pope